The Hat Industry of Luton and its Buildings

The Hat Industry of Luton and its Buildings

Katie Carmichael, David McOmish and David Grech

ENGLISH HERITAGE

Front cover
Better known today as 'The Hat Factory' arts centre, J & K Connor Ltd's hat factory on Bute Street, Luton, is shown shortly after opening in 1927, as photographed by Bedford Lemere & Co.
[BL29379_004]

Inside cover
Some of the thousands of plaster hat forms carved by hand at Boon & Lane Ltd in Luton which are used to create the aluminium hat blocks upon which hats are shaped.
[DP153620]

Frontispiece
Although Luton was known as the home of ladies' straw hat manufacture, hats of all styles and materials were made – including straw policemen's helmets for summer use.
[Getty Images /Hulton Archive]

Published by English Heritage, The Engine House, Fire Fly Avenue, Swindon SN2 2EH
www.english-heritage.org.uk
English Heritage is the Government's lead body for the historic environment.

First published 2013

ISBN 978-1-84802-119-8

Product code 51750

British Library Cataloguing in Publication data
A CIP catalogue record for this book is available from the British Library.

Typeset in Charter ITC 9.5/13pt.

Brought to publication by Rachel Howard, Publishing, English Heritage.

Edited by Susan Kelleher
Page layout by Anthony Cohen
Photographs by Steve Cole, Derek Kendall, Katie Carmichael and David Grech, English Heritage
Graphics by Allan T Adams and Philip Sinton
Printed in the UK by Park Communications Ltd.

Contents

Acknowledgements

We would like to express our gratitude for the assistance and support provided by our colleagues in English Heritage. The graphics were produced by Allan T Adams and Philip Sinton; and, with the exception of those taken by the authors, the photographs were taken by Steve Cole and Derek Kendall. Additional thanks are due to Peter Guillery, Kathryn Morrison and Roger M Thomas for commenting on the text.

The assistance of the following individuals was invaluable: Elizabeth Adey, Chris Grabham and Veronica Main (of Luton Culture), Gemma Pike (Luton Borough Council), and Wesley Keir (Albion Archaeology).

We would like to thank the individuals, local history societies, local interest groups and heritage forums for their interest, assistance and time. Colchester and Ipswich Museums allowed us access to their collections and to photograph items for use as illustrations, whilst Luton Culture and Hitchin Museum (currently accessed through the British Schools Museum) also allowed us to use images from their collection.

We are grateful to all the members of the public who responded to our requests for information posted on social networks and blogs, and published in newsletters and newspapers – the information that we received was invaluable and although we weren't able to include all of the information we received it helped us to gain a far greater understanding of the subject than would otherwise have been possible. Linda Kilpatrick, in particular, must be thanked for allowing us to reproduce her memories of her time in Luton. Similarly, the Hewitt and Ackroyd families were kind enough to allow use to use family documents and pictures.

We would especially like to thank all the householders and business owners who generously gave us access to their properties and supplied historical information. Special thanks must be given to Boon & Lane Ltd for allowing us to interrupt their daily routine on several occasions in order to undertake photography and filming, and to K R Snoxell & Sons Ltd, Walter Wright Ltd and Barford Brothers Ltd.

Foreword

'Heritage' is unlikely to be the first word that one associates with Luton. Certainly, many people think of Luton as a new town, but our work and other recent studies reveal a Luton with ancient roots. There is clear evidence for long-hidden Anglo-Saxon settlement and burials – indeed, there may well be Roman settlement here too – and by the Middle Ages the importance of Luton as a thriving market town in the Chilterns, and as an important ecclesiastical hub, was reinforced by the presence of not one, but two castles.

Whilst to most people Luton is understandably associated with the motor car, the successful establishment of the Vauxhall factory here in 1905 was due in no small part to the existing technological and artistic skills of the local workforce. Luton and its surrounding towns and villages were once the beating heart of an internationally important industry specialising in the manufacture of ladies' hats. The levels of production were astounding – at one stage, in the 1930s, the region was producing over 70 million hats each year – but, with shifting economic fortunes and changing tastes in fashion, the industry entered a period of rapid decline from which it never fully recovered.

Although the industry is deeply embedded in local consciousness – celebrated in the town crest and in the name of Luton's football team, 'The Hatters' – and its historical importance recognised by local interest groups for some time, it has been largely overlooked by the country at large. Our work in the region over the past few years has sought to provide a sharper understanding of the significance and value of the surviving historic fabric relating to the manufacture of straw and felt hats and to find ways of presenting that to a new and wider audience.

The hat industry has undoubtedly left a mark on the landscape of the region and many fine buildings associated with the trade remain. It is, however, a bittersweet inheritance – the impact of economic and social changes in the 20th century means that empty buildings and run-down areas can be seen throughout the town. This has resulted in a completely understandable response which has tended to focus on piecemeal clearance and rebuilding – rather than repair – as a means of revitalisation, and many buildings of interest have already been lost. The character of former hat-working areas can be eroded by new developments, and once lost cannot be reinstated. We hope that a fresh understanding and appreciation of Luton's industrial heritage will encourage local placemakers to work together and that they will put buildings associated with hat making at the centre of future regeneration schemes, thus upholding the identity and distinctiveness of the town. We believe that these remaining buildings, and the stories that they tell about the lives of ordinary people, should be a source of civic pride for everyone locally, regardless of age, ethnicity or social background, and are worthy of national recognition.

Simon Thurley
Chief Executive of English Heritage

HAT FAC. (E.M.)
590
STRAW HAT FAC. (E.M.)
TRIMMINGS WHSE
REST.
STRAW HAT WHSE. & FAC.
TRIMMING WHSE.
PLAIT WHSE.
9
10
TINGSMITH
PLAIT STORE
RIBBONS STORE
FELT
STA.
PLAIT WHSE.
STRAW HAT FAC. & WHSE.
HAT WHSE. & FAC. (E.M.)
604
602
598
600
640
638
641
639
HATS
CURRANT & CREEK
SHOWROOMS
CONCRETE FLOORS
LOUVRE
STONE STAIRS
LANE
1929

1 Introduction

Luton is a remarkable place – an energetic and youthful town which owes its current social and ethnic diversity, as well as a legacy of declining industry, to massive growth in the 19th and early 20th centuries. The town has been dominated by a Vauxhall plant since 1905, but its industrial roots run much deeper. Long before it became associated with motor cars, Luton was well established as an international centre of hat making.

More specifically, Luton was the main centre of ladies' hat production in the UK for over 200 years, with surrounding towns and villages across Bedfordshire, Hertfordshire, Buckinghamshire and Essex feeding into the industry and helping to make the region globally renowned. This success was founded on the earlier regional industry of straw plaiting, an occupation that was well established by the late 17th century (Fig 1). Straw plaiting received a boost during the Napoleonic Wars of 1803–15, when supplies of straw plait from Italy – which had a long-established industry producing high-quality plaits in fashionable designs – were cut off and hefty import duties were imposed. As a result, the industry underwent rapid expansion: subsequently 80 per cent of all straw plaiters in the country (around 22,000 people by 1851) were based in the south-east Midlands, with 50 per cent of those living in southern Bedfordshire. Luton became the commercial hub of the industry and was transformed from a thinly populated rural township into an industrial centre in a remarkably short period of time. Elsewhere, in the outlying towns and villages, much of the work continued to be carried out on a domestic scale.

The importation of cheap foreign plaits in the 1870s led to the decline of the local plaiting industry and, subsequently, less focus on the manufacture of straw hats and an increasing shift towards general hat manufacture, an industry which made greater use of large factory and warehouse buildings – although domestic-scale workshops continued to be a marked feature of the trade.

At its peak in the 1930s, the region was producing as many as 70 million hats in a single year but, following the Second World War, it entered a rapid decline from which it never fully recovered. This has left Luton, Dunstable and a number of other local towns with a challenging inheritance of neglected and decaying fragments of a once vital industry (Fig 2). These need to be understood if they are to be successfully incorporated within future regeneration plans.

Luton was once home to a remarkable concentration of hat factories, warehouses and associated services, as seen in this extract from a Goad fire insurance plan of 1932. [© database right Landmark Information Group Ltd. (All rights reserved 2013)]

Figure 1
A depiction of a straw plaiter as seen in The Illustrated London News, *29 March 1884. Plaiters were highly skilled and in a good year could earn considerable sums of money. However, prices fluctuated wildly and most found it necessary to plait almost constantly in order to make ends meet – indeed, girls could often be seen plaiting as they walked.*

Figure 2
Dusty bowler hats sit forgotten inside Boon & Lane Ltd, a blockmakers on Taylor Street, Luton. Changing fashions and fortunes have led to a decline in the UK trade and an upsurge in imports from the Far East, putting many firms out of business and forcing others to adapt.
[DP153643]

In response to mounting development pressure in the region, English Heritage carried out an Historic Area Assessment of the Plaiters' Lea Conservation Area in Luton, which was published in 2011. This book aims to augment the Area Assessment by examining the broader industry, exploring the evolution of plaiting and hat making in the region and highlighting the significance of the surviving fabric and its role in conservation and regeneration. These are key elements in the National Planning Policy Framework which stresses the need to develop a positive strategy for the conservation and enjoyment of the historic environment, including heritage assets most at risk through neglect, decay or other threats.

L
U
T
O
N
1420
1419
1418
1417
1414
1413
1412
1411
1410
1392
1409
1684
1685
1686
1687
1672
1671
1667
1448
1473
1471
1121
1122
1123
1124
1117
1116
1115
1114
1113
387
388
1088
1089
1091
1087
1086
1085
1084
1083
1735
1734
1740
1767
1766
1642
1604
1601
1603
1600
1602
1597
1596

2

Historic and regional development

Luton is synonymous with hat making. The industry is woven into the core fabric of the town and, despite its collapse in the middle of the 20th century, the history of hat making continues to be a matter of great civic pride. Indeed, the crest of Luton Town Football Club incorporates a sheaf of straw and a straw hat and the team's nickname, 'The Hatters', is a reworking of their earlier name 'Straw Plaiters'. A parliamentary debate in 1999 – the designated 'Year of the Hat' – led by the then MP for Luton South, Margaret Moran, underscored the historical significance of hat making to communities in Bedfordshire, particularly Luton, and concluded with a plea for support for hat making in the town and area:

> To cap it all, I would like to thank my hon. Friend the Minister [for Energy and Industry, Mr John Battle] for attending the debate. I hope that he, too, will encourage and support the Luton hat industry. We are not all as mad as hatters in trying to promote the industry. It is a serious industry providing many jobs, especially for women, as well as much enjoyment, entertainment and pleasure, as many of my hon. Friends here today have demonstrated.[1]

Evidently, this plea fell on deaf ears, and not only are the specialist skills of plaiting and hat making disappearing fast (Fig 3), so too are the factories, warehouses and showrooms which formed the rich architectural heritage of the trade (Figs 4 and 5).

Despite the emblematic and iconic status of hats and hat making in the region, these activities were not confined to Luton and its immediate environs. Other national centres of production existed in Stockport, Cheshire and London, whereas local foci of industry were to be found throughout Bedfordshire, Buckinghamshire, Hertfordshire and even into Essex. The development of the industry in this region is borne of a complex set of varied circumstances – historical, social and agricultural – which encouraged an essentially low-key cottage industry to expand rapidly into a global enterprise.

Many of the towns and large villages within the region were, to a greater or lesser degree, engaged with the preparation and production of straw plaits or the making of hats – particularly Luton, Dunstable, St Albans, Aylesbury,

Luton on the brink of expansion: a tithe map of 1844 showing the existing road pattern to the south of the River Lea, with proposed new roads on the north. [Luton Culture]

Figure 3
A sewer at K R Snoxell & Sons Ltd, 24–26 Clarendon Road, Luton, uses a specially designed sewing machine to finish the brims on hats. Much early machinery remains in use and little changed, testament to their effectiveness. The ribbons being used were dyed just a few streets away, at the Barford Brothers' dye works on North Street. [DP153723]

Figure 4
The interior of Boon & Lane blockmakers on Taylor Street, Luton. Boon & Lane employs just two people and is the last example of a traditional industry which once employed thousands of men throughout the region. [DP153606]

Figure 5
The showroom of K R Snoxell & Sons Ltd. Famed for making the 'Luton Civic Boater', so named because they were supplied to the local council, the firm moved to Clarendon Road in the 1950s, moving from number 22 to its present address (24–26) in the 1990s. It continues to manufacture boaters, as well as a variety of other designs. [DP153713]

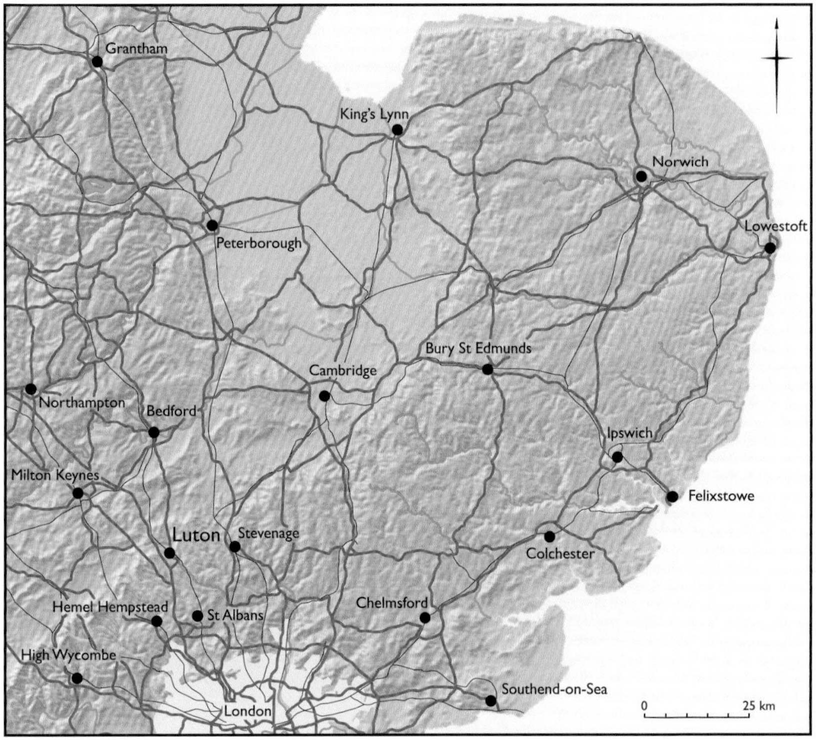

Figure 6
This book focuses on the hatting and related industries across a large swathe of eastern England, to the north of the Thames Valley. The soils in this area reflect the underlying geology which is dominated by chalk, but with substantial tracts of clay too. These, together with an advantageous climate, have proven ideal for the cultivation of wheat and thus ensured that there was a ready supply of good quality straw for use in the plaiting, and then hat-making, industries. Proximity to London and other large market centres was exploited by manufacturers and suppliers, especially when rail links were established in the middle decades of the 19th century.

Berkhamsted, Hemel Hempstead, Hitchin, Markyate, Redbourn, and Tring (Fig 6). These towns are set within a landscape which is dominated by the high chalk ridge of the Chilterns, 'The Delectable Mountains' in John Bunyan's *The Pilgrim's Progress* (1678).

The Chilterns played a crucial role in the development of settlement patterns throughout the region. The channels carved through this natural barrier by glacial meltwater and streams served as natural foci for the establishment of settlements and trade routes (Fig 7). One of the best known routes in the Chilterns, the Icknield Way, long held to be a trackway established in the Neolithic period, has, in all likelihood, a post-Roman origin but a number of major Roman roads pass through the region, including Watling Street (the A5 from London, passing through Dunstable) and Akeman Street

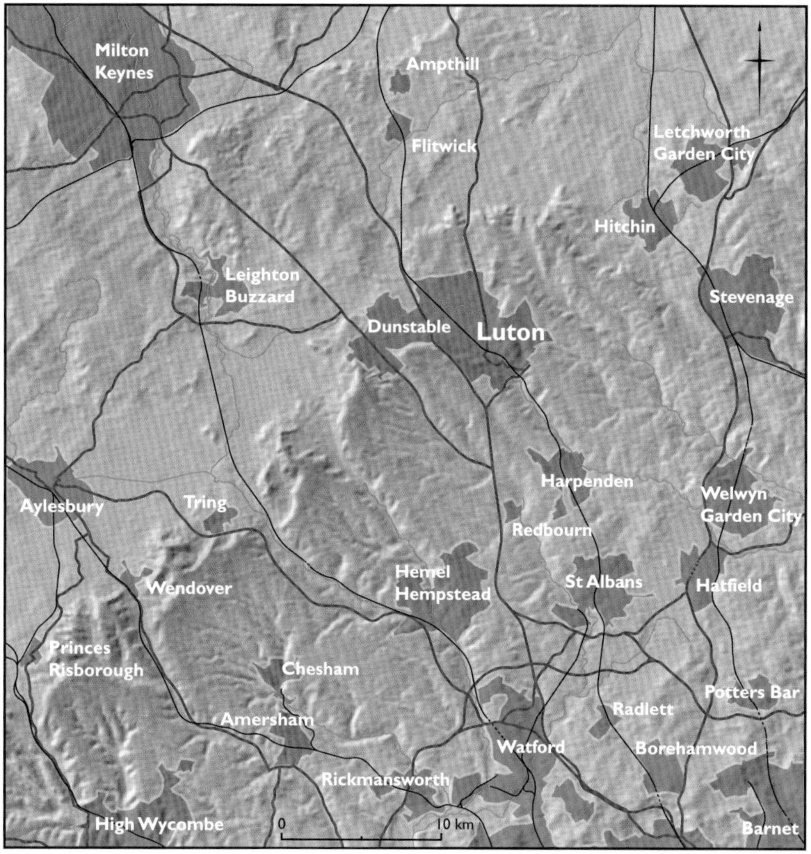

Figure 7
The band of chalk shown running SW–NE is the Chilterns Ridge. A dominant feature in the landscape, many of the largest towns lie at the foot of the scarp slope to the north or on the shallower dipslopes to the south, with a number of others developing in the gaps cut through the chalk by river valleys and which subsequently became important trade routes. Many of these towns, such as Luton and St Albans, were significant settlements, market centres and ecclesiastical hubs in the medieval period.

(the A41 from St Albans to Aylesbury). These were connected to a network of lesser tracks and lanes servicing smaller urban and commercial centres.

Accordingly, the archaeological record in the region is rich. Pleistocene artefacts and fauna, at least 250,000 years old, have been found at Caddington to the south of Luton (Fig 8). Recent work here suggests that deeply buried in situ deposits of this date, or older, also survive in the vicinity. Some Palaeolithic and Mesolithic material has been found in and around Luton, but most finds date from the fourth millennium BC onwards. At this time it is clear that people started to commemorate individuals and communities by

Figure 8
The eminent antiquarian, Worthington George Smith, at work in the quarry at Caddington in the final decade of the 19th century. He was a remarkable character, also celebrated as a naturalist, but his work on the early archaeology of the area is renowned. His exploration of local quarries and claypits led to the discovery of a number of important, and rare, Palaeolithic sites – largely dating to the Ipswichian inter-glacial, c *135,000–110,000 years ago.*
[Luton Culture]

Figure 9
Maiden Bower, seen in the bottom-right of the photograph and a prominent local landmark, is a prehistoric enclosure which sits at the north-facing edge of the Chiltern scarp on the western fringes of Dunstable. A single oval circuit of bank and ditch, dating to the Iron Age, can be seen but this has been built over, and so masks, a much older ceremonial site – a causewayed enclosure that was constructed as early as 3775 cal BC.
[NMR 26524/01]

constructing large elongated and circular burial mounds such as those on the Dunstable Downs and Galley Hill on the northern outskirts of Luton. A circular ceremonial centre at Maiden Bower, Dunstable (Fig 9), was in use between *c* 3800 and 3200 BC; whilst the enclosure at Waulud's Bank, just to the north of Luton town centre, dates to the middle of the third millennium BC.

The towns of the hat industry

As well as the long-established settlement of St Albans (Roman *Verulamium)*, a major mercantile centre and settlement emerged at Dunstable, on the route of Watling Street, and at Luton. Founded upon their earlier success as market towns, these three settlements would come to dominate the 19th- and 20th-century trades of straw plaiting and hat making.

Spending time in these places today it is sometimes easy to overlook their historic character, but on closer examination it is still possible to tease out older street patterns which reveal the extent of the earlier settlements, dominated by their former medieval marketplaces, and with Roman or even prehistoric origins.

St Albans is often cited as the oldest town in England and it is clear that a substantial settlement, possibly the tribal capital of the *Catuvellauni,* was established during the middle decades of the first century BC and called *Verlamion* ('place by the marsh'). Inscribed, pre-Roman, coins were minted here and its significance was enhanced after the Claudian Conquest of AD 43; its importance underscored by the fact that it was targeted during the Boudiccan Revolt of AD 60.

The overall extent of the Roman town is uncertain but it centred on the area now outlined by Verulamium Park and was defined by a series of defences, which culminated in the 4th century AD with the construction of a significant enclosing wall. Although not deserted, the town had become largely abandoned by the end of the 5th century in favour of another local settlement, Kingsbury; but the foundation of a Benedictine abbey in 793 AD by King Offa in honour of St Alban (derived from the name of a *Verulamium* resident martyred because of his Christian faith) acted as a catalyst for renewed urban development as a settlement grew up around the monastic precinct.

The importance of St Albans as a regional market centre grew throughout the medieval period, underscored by its royal and ecclesiastical connections as well as its proximity to London (Fig 10).

Dunstable, although considerably smaller than St Albans, has an extensive and complex history. There is good evidence for prehistoric activity in and around what later developed as the modern-day town, and a major settlement was established here, probably at a crossing point on Watling Street, in the Roman period. Surprisingly little is known about the form and extent of the town thereafter. It may well have been one of a number of towns destroyed during late 9th-century Danish raids, suffering the same fate again in 1010, but by the early 1100s a planned market town had been built which included, in 1123, a royal residence on what is now Church Street, used by Henry I as a base on his hunting visits to the area.

Dunstable Priory was founded in 1131 by the king and in the same year a town charter was granted to the priors. Dunstable was also one of a number of sites where Eleanor of Castile's coffin was put on public display on its route to London in 1290. A cross to commemorate this was erected the following year and a modern memorial has been placed in the shopping centre on the High Street. Throughout the medieval period Dunstable was clearly a town of some importance, with a large marketplace and extensive urban development (Fig 11).

Nearby Luton is a settlement of marked historical significance with Saxon origins: the name of *Lygetune* suggests an enclosed or defended farm/homestead on the River Lea. Judging by subsequent references, Luton and its hinterland provided a regular arena for frequent territorial quarrels between competing fiefdoms. One Anglo-Saxon Chronicle entry dated 871 AD places Luton on the boundary in a settlement dispute between Alfred and the Danish leader, Guthrum, and additional entries record a successful defence of the town in response to an attack by the Danes in 913 AD.

The town is referred to as *Loitoine* in the Domesday Book, the manor listed as being among the king's lands, and it remained in the hands of the Crown until it was granted to Robert, Earl of Gloucester, by Henry I early in the 12th century. It was subsequently given to a foreign mercenary, Robert de Waudari, by Stephen in 1139 in retaliation for Gloucester's support of Matilda during the Anarchy. Waudari built a wooden castle on high ground overlooking the town

Figure 10
A view of St Albans Cathedral in 1920. In the foreground, in close proximity to the cathedral, is a long, narrow building – one of the town's many hat factories which have since disappeared.
[EPW001251]

Figure 11
Dunstable's High Street and marketplace as viewed from the east in 1928.
[EPW023863]

to the south, but it was briefly occupied and dismantled 15 years later under the terms of a truce. A second castle, in a different location, was built by Fulk de Breauté in 1221 but, again, this was short-lived and destroyed in 1224 or 1225.

Much of the medieval building stock in Luton was destroyed in the 'Great Fire' which swept through the town in 1336, erasing its early urban form. It was probably a linear settlement along the High Street, now known as George Street, stretching from the area occupied by the Town Hall south-east to Castle Hill and the Law Courts.

For much of the medieval period, Luton served as a market town and ecclesiastical centre for a large, rural, hinterland. The outline of the marketplace, on George Street, is still visible, and the layout of the modern town in this area probably reflects its medieval origins too.

3 Straw plaiting

'The hat industry' is a somewhat artificial term which encompasses two quite separate, but often co-dependent, industries: straw plaiting and hat making. Hat making itself should not be confused with millinery proper which is more concerned with the finishing of hats rather than the complete manufacturing process for which Luton was to become so well known.

Origins of the industry

The hat industry around Luton was founded upon the success of one material – straw. This basic material would come to dominate the lives of tens of thousands of individuals throughout the region as, in the hands of a skilled worker, it was transformed from a simple cereal crop into functional, sometimes artistic, headwear.

Basic straw hats have been used for millennia and the origins of working straw into plaits before sewing them together to form a hat remain unknown. Several European locations lay claim to the process – the Geer valley near Liege in central Belgium is said to have an industry dating from the Middle Ages; in the German republic of Saxony it may date from the 16th century, whilst in Florence the industry was well enough established by 1575 to warrant a corporation of straw-hat merchants.

Popular belief has it that the introduction of straw plaiting to Britain may be attributed to Mary I of Scotland, who is said to have brought craftsmen over from her mother's birthplace of Lorraine and established them in Scotland. Her son, James I of England, is then said to have settled them in the south of England upon his accession in 1603, leaving them under the care of the Napier family – then owners of Luton Hoo, a grand country estate and house lying to the south-east of Luton.

This may be fanciful, but what is certain is that straw plaiting had become an important rural industry by 1689 when the inhabitants of Bedfordshire, Buckinghamshire and Hertfordshire petitioned Parliament to reject a proposed bill forcing people to wear wool-felt hats – it was claimed that such a bill would ruin nearly 1,000 families in the area, affecting more than 14,000 individuals who relied on straw plaiting.

During the Napoleonic Wars (1803–15), supplies of Leghorn plait from

Straw plait came in many different designs, most of them reasonably simple, like these examples, but expensive hats made use of intricate plaits of differing colours and textures.
[With the permission of Colchester and Ipswich Museums]

Italy were cut off and expensive tariffs imposed on all other imported plaits and hats. The result of this was a rise in locally produced plaits and hats as manufacturers turned to alternative sources. Some Luton hat manufacturers bought their straw plait directly from French prisoners of war interred at Yaxley Barracks near Peterborough (Fig 12) where the first straw-splitters – a simple device which allowed straws to be split into several splints before being plaited – were said to have been used, resulting in a finer and far superior plait.

Figure 12
A painting by Arthur Claude Cooke, created in 1909, showing plait merchants dealing with French prisoners of war at Norman Cross, or Yaxley Barracks, near Peterborough. A pile of plait can be seen in the lower left corner whilst, to the right, a guard turns a blind eye to the ongoing trade.
[Luton Culture]

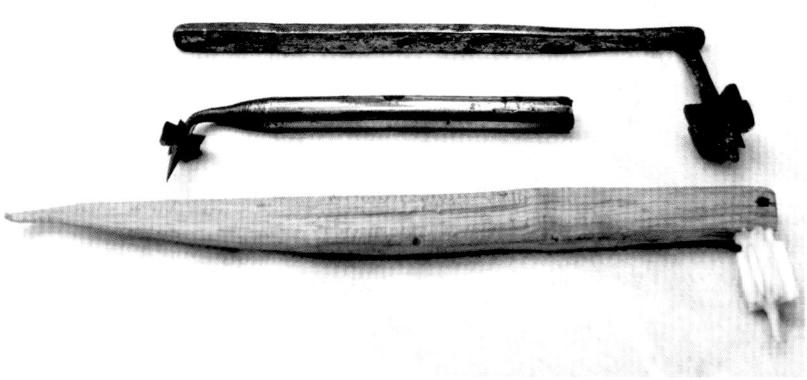

Figure 13
The industry was once prevalent as far east as Essex, as evidenced by this selection of bone- and metal-handled straw-splitters held in the collections of the Colchester Museum Service. Made first from bone and later from metal, these simple devices were inserted into the ends of a straw in order to split it into a number of equally sized splints.
[With the permission of Colchester and Ipswich Museums]

Although this trade was banned by the authorities, many of the guards at the camp were complicit in the smuggling – such was the demand in Luton that the financial rewards presumably made the risk worthwhile. A steadier source was needed, but the quality of the locally produced plait had for many years been deemed an inferior product when compared with fine Tuscan plait.

This issue was largely resolved following the widespread introduction of the straw-splitter in the 19th century (Fig 13), resulting in a fine plait which could compete with those from the continent and leading to a boom in the straw-plaiting industry which developed from a cottage industry into a large-scale industrial venture during the course of the century. The coming of the railways encouraged an already growing industry to develop further, with many former coaching inns in towns such as Dunstable freed up for use as hat factories.

It is commonly held that a formal straw-plaiting industry developed in and around Dunstable before similar developments in Luton, and that the industry spread from Bedfordshire into Hertfordshire. A parliamentary report of 1817, however, includes the testimony of William Wilshere, magistrate for Hertford and Bedford, who implied the reverse, describing the trade of straw plaiting as 'considerable in Hertfordshire and now it is becoming general in Bedfordshire … I speak of the present moment, and it has been extending for ten years'.[2]

Whilst the straw-plaiting industry in the south of England was very much focused in Bedfordshire and Hertfordshire, it also provided employment across a broader swathe of the country – including Essex. The Essex trade is unusual in that it is known to have been artificially introduced to the area at the end of the 18th century by the Marquis and Marchioness of Buckingham, who lived at Gosfield Hall near Halstead (Fig 14). In an effort to bolster the local economy by providing employment for the poor following the decline of the worsted spinning industry, the Buckinghams hired an instructor from Dunstable to teach local women the art of plaiting. Although the Buckinghams were partially successful, the industry remained confined to the Colne Valley and the Braintree district, the closest plait market being that in Hitchin, Hertfordshire, some 50 miles distant.

Figure 14
Gosfield Hall, near Halstead in Essex, was one of the homes of the Marquis and Marchioness of Buckingham who are credited with introducing the straw-plaiting industry to Essex at the end of the 18th century in a bid to bolster the local economy.
[BB047330]

Despite best efforts, competition with Italian plait remained sharp and the reintroduction of goods from Switzerland and Saxony in the mid-19th century saw the English plaiting industry contract to a nucleus in Hertfordshire and Bedfordshire. Why the straw-hatting industry became centred in this region is open to debate, but three key factors may have been influential – the availability of large areas of cheap land for development, the presence of entrepreneurs willing to exploit an emerging market, all underpinned by the silica-rich qualities of the soils here, which helped to produce strong yet flexible straws ideal for plaiting.

Plaiting

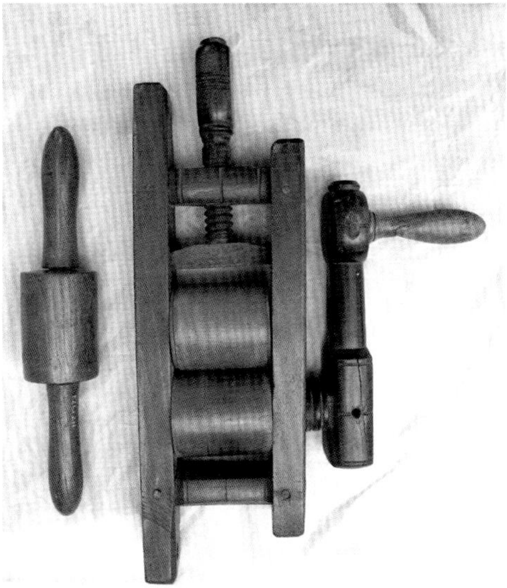

Figure 15
A splint-mill and a hand-roller, both used for softening and flattening straw splints prior to them being plaited. A plait-mill looked very similar to a splint-mill, but the rollers had a groove at one end to prevent the decorative head of the plait from being crushed.
[With the permission of Colchester and Ipswich Museums]

The process by which straws were turned into plaits is simultaneously straightforward and ingenious. The first step was the preparation of the raw material – all leaves and knots were removed from the straws before they were trimmed to around 10in (250mm) in length; the straws would then be bleached – at first using the fumes from molten sulphur, and later, in the factories, with the use of hydrogen peroxide which had the advantage of removing minor discolorations as well as bleaching the straw.

Once cleaned, the straws would be graded according to size through the use of a straw-sorter, a wooden casing fitted with a graduated series of meshes allowing the straws to fall into separate containers, after which they would be tied into bundles about 6in (150mm) in diameter ready for sale by the straw dealers.

From around 1800 it became increasingly common to split whole straws into a number of narrow splints by the use of a straw-splitter. Before they could be made ready for plaiting the splints would be softened in a splint-mill – a wooden mangle which could be attached to a door frame (Fig 15).

Straw plaiters worked with a bundle of straws or splints under the left arm (*see* Fig 1), each straw being moistened between the lips before being worked into the plait. As new straws were continually fed into the developing plait the ends of these would be clipped off before the plait was completed.

Plaits varied greatly in design, quality, width and the number of straws or splints used to create them. One of the advantages of using straw splints was that the outer and inner side of a straw differ in colour and texture – the inner part being whiter and more matt in appearance, thus allowing for a greater variety of patterns when used in contrast to the outer side. Plaits could be anything from a 3-end to a 16-end plait or more, although plaits made using 7 straws were the most commonly used. A fine Leghorn plait would normally use 13 straws – generally speaking the more straws used and the more complex the design, the greater the price that could be obtained.

After the plait had reached the required length – commonly 20yd (18m) – it was passed through a plait-mill, similar in construction to a splint-mill but with grooved rollers to prevent the decorative head of the plait from being crushed – the milling being carried out in the factories or sewing rooms (Fig 16).

Figure 16
A depiction of a bonnet sewing room by W Hatherell, late 19th century. Women and children sew straw hats by hand – on the wall on the right is a series of plait-mills, wooden rollers used to press plait flat before it was sewn. [Luton Culture, from the collection of Thomas Wyatt Bagshawe]

Child labour

The extent to which the plaiting industry relied upon children is revealed by the establishment of plaiting schools around Luton at the start of the 19th century. Children were generally taught the basics of plaiting at home before being sent to a plait school between the ages of three and four when their work was considered to be financially viable. Even younger children could be found in the schools and, although unable to plait, children as young as two might be tasked with clipping the loose ends of straws. At least 10,000 children are believed to have attended such schools in Bedfordshire at any given point during the first half of the 19th century, with as many as 13,000 attending during the peak years of the industry.

Figure 17
Young girls plait straws outside their house in Titmore Green near Hitchin, Hertfordshire. Children would normally be taught how to plait at the age of three or four and their earnings formed a considerable part of a family's income.
[North Hertfordshire Museum Service]

The schools charged weekly fees of 2d or 3d, and the children would be expected to earn between 9d a week aged eight to as much as 3s a week by the age of 14. Although straw plaiting could be done outside (Fig 17), and the children were therefore able to get some fresh air, it also meant that they were expected to work on their plait almost constantly – even when walking. Accordingly, older children were expected to produce around 30yd (27m) of plait a day, and an interview by the Assistant Commissioner for the Children's Employment Commission in 1863–4 with a four-year-old girl called Mary Scrivener in Houghton Regis reveals that she was expected to produce 10yd (9m) of plait in a six-hour working day.[3]

Although called 'schools' these institutions were, in fact, little more than workshops where the master's or mistress's sole duty was to oversee the work of the children. Many of the mistresses could not even read or write, some could not even plait, and rather than teaching the children to read many of them simply taught the children to memorise passages from the Bible.

Conditions in the schools were often deplorable, with reports of up to 60 children in a room a little over 10ft (3m) square, and another of 30 children in a room measuring just 14ft by 7ft (4.3m by 2.1m) – open fires would be too dangerous in such crowded rooms, so the only heat during winter came from small charcoal 'dick-pots' – a type of brazier. Although child plaiters were generally safer and healthier than many children employed in other industries, especially in the textile mills of the North, the practice of drawing straws through the mouth before they could be set into the plait was said to cause sores on the lips as well as associated stomach problems and catarrhal diseases.

One notable exception appears to be the plait school which was built on Old Watling Street equidistant between Flamstead and Markyate (Fig 18), which was unusual not only in being purpose-built, but also for teaching the children to read, write and count to an acceptable standard. The focus on a balance between academic and practical lessons may be largely attributed to the influence of the Sebright family of Beechwood Park, which lies less than two miles to the south of Markyate. When the 7th baronet died in 1846 he bequeathed an endowment for the building and running of 'The Sebright School' at Cheverell's Green on the southern edge of Markyate. The school was built in 1866 and existed to further the religious education of the local children, who graduated from the plait school on Watling Street to the Sebright School. Clearly, there was a strong connection between the two schools and as there was a 20-year period between the endowment being made and the new school opening, it would appear that the Sebright trustees took a keen interest in the standards of education at the plait school.

Figure 18
A former plait school situated on the old Watling Street between Flamstead and Markyate in Hertfordshire. It is rare to find a purpose-built example and this building is especially unusual for being constructed in rat-trap bond, a way of building walls in which bricks are placed on their sides. Since this type of bond uses fewer bricks than a standard bond it is much cheaper, but also less stable and is often reserved for non-load-bearing walls in gardens. [DP153731]

In 1867 the Government passed the Workshop Regulation Act which banned the employment of children under the age of 8, and required children aged between 8 and 13 to attend school for a minimum of 10 hours a week. Initially, there was some confusion as to whether the plait schools fell within the provisions of the Act, and it quickly became evident that the number of children employed in this manner made it very difficult for the factory inspectors to enforce the law. The Act was met with great resistance in the region, where it was argued that children needed to learn the skill whilst young if they were to obtain any degree of proficiency in their work, one sub-inspector even admitting that:

> Certain manipulations requiring nimbleness of fingers, if not learnt and mastered at a young age, cannot be learnt at all. If the Workshops Act of 1867 could and would be enforced according to the letter, it would probably have the effect of exterminating the plait and pillow-lace trades altogether.[4]

Accordingly, no strict attempt was made to enforce the law in the region until the Luton School Board brought its first case for non-attendance at school to court on 4 June 1875, spelling the beginning of the end for plaiting schools.

Economic and regional impact

For those living within a roughly 25-mile radius of Luton in the middle of the 19th century, the rural economy was dominated by straw plaiting (Fig 19). The census returns reveal that at the peak of the industry in 1871 there were 20,701 plaiters in Bedfordshire and 12,089 in Hertfordshire, with around 15 per cent of all females in Bedfordshire declaring themselves as straw plaiters, and with 25–30 per cent of those being between 5 and 14 years of age. These numbers probably under-represent the true extent of the plaiting industry as many women and children worked only on a part-time basis and would not necessarily have declared their work.

Although straw plaiting was primarily the occupation of women and children, men were known to take it up for part of the year to supplement their

agricultural wages. Its small profit margins, however, did not often warrant the financial investment required to build workshops and most of the work was simply carried out in the home (Fig 20). Consequently, plaiters were generally independent and self-employed, buying bundles of straw directly from straw merchants and selling their completed plait to plait merchants, who would in turn sell the plait to hat manufacturers at the local markets. A small number of straw plaiters sold their wares directly at the markets in the hope of securing a better price, but at the expense of losing a day's labour.

Markets were held at Luton, Hitchin (Fig 21), Hemel Hempstead, Berkhamsted, Tring, Chesham, Dunstable, Leighton Buzzard and St Albans. Most of the markets opened at 9am, before which time it was illegal to trade. The reality, however, was a little different. At Hitchin market and elsewhere a system of hand signals developed which allowed many deals between plaiters and dealers to be agreed by the time the market opened. It was a simple system whereby the plait dealer would hold a certain number of fingers by his side – say perhaps four – to indicate how many shillings he was willing to

Figure 19 (above left)
Straw plaiting sometimes provided for entire communities whose lives were dependent on the trade – including the residents of Hollow Lane in Hitchin, many of whom can be seen with plait in this photograph. [North Hertfordshire Museum Service]

Figure 20 (above right)
Charlotte Norris is seen plaiting in her house in Slip End, Hertfordshire, in this photograph (of c 1894) taken by Frederick Thurston. Although the local straw-plaiting industry was largely extinct by this time there are reports of elderly women continuing to plait into the 1930s. [Private collection]

Figure 21
A large part of Hitchin's market was given over to the buying and selling of plait, seen here neatly arranged in bundles in the women's arms, and attracted traders from as far afield as Essex.
[Luton Culture]

pay; if the plaiter looked towards the clock on the church then the deal had been declined, if not, the deal had been accepted. By this means no words were needed, and the dealer did not even need to pause in his supposed perambulations of the market.

Luton's existing Market House was in a parlous condition by the 1860s and the Monday plait market necessitated the closure of George Street to all through traffic. Consequently, the local Board of Health voted in favour of the construction of dedicated plait halls on Cheapside and Waller Street in 1869. These interconnected buildings with their fixed counters and plait racks were considered a great improvement upon the open-air market as they allowed the larger plait dealers to display their goods without fear of rain damage (Fig 22). Upwards of 2,000 buyers and sellers could be accommodated comfortably, whilst the authorities could better monitor proceedings. Hitchin and Dunstable followed suit in 1874, but Hitchin's plait hall was short-lived, closing in 1898.

One of the most marked features of the straw-plaiting industry was its seasonality – the harvest and fashion seasons necessarily dictating the rhythms of the trade. The price for plait in spring and summer was double that of autumn or winter. The earnings of straw plaiters therefore varied according to the season, but the average earnings over the course of a year in the mid-19th century were somewhere in the region of 5s a week, compared to 10s a week for an agricultural labourer.

Figure 22
A plait dealer displays his wares in Luton's purpose-built Waller Street plait market, in 1885. The sign above the stall is formed from plait and the counter is decorated with 5¼-mile reels of thread used by hat-sewing machines.
[Luton Culture]

Given that straw plaiting was generally a home-based activity, unaffected by the weather or the hours of natural light available, it was often seized upon by those with political or social agendas as being responsible for women disregarding their domestic duties – supposedly resulting in dirty homes and neglected children. Additionally, the extra earnings made by the women and children were said to have made the men lazy and happy to rely on their families rather than find regular employment.

Decline

The plait industry was relatively short-lived. It was still flourishing in *c* 1880 but it then entered a period of rapid decline until, by the time of the 1901 census, there were only 485 plaiters in Bedfordshire – 98 per cent fewer than 30 years previously – and 681 in Hertfordshire, a reduction of some 94 per cent.

By 1893 it was estimated that less than 5 per cent of the plait sold at Luton market was English and the industry was all but extinct in most of the surrounding towns and villages. The sharp decline in straw plaiting was linked to the rising number of imported plaits from China and Japan – these cheap imports had reduced the price manufacturers were willing to pay for plait and made the work increasingly unprofitable. Increasing numbers of plaiters, mainly women, moved to Luton from the surrounding villages and took up work in the more lucrative business of straw hat and bonnet sewing. Old habits were hard to break, however, and there are reports of women continuing to plait long after the industry had supposedly disappeared – such as the case of Miss Sexton of Tilehouse Street, Hitchin, who could be seen seated just inside her doorway, working at her plait as late as 1923.

ENGLAND

4

Hat manufacture and trade

The manufacturing of hats was not unique to the Luton region; hats were also produced in London, the Denton and Stockport areas of Greater Manchester, and Atherstone in Warwickshire, with each place tending to specialise in a particular aspect of the industry. Hat manufacturing could take one of two forms: the straw-hat trade focused on the production of women's hats and bonnets, whilst the fur- and wool-felt trade concentrated on the manufacture of caps and men's hats. Denton, Stockport and Atherstone formed the centre of the felt trade whilst Luton began as the centre of the straw-hat trade before turning to wool-felt, with London, although home to a few fur-felt manufactures, largely focusing on the finishing and millinery aspects of the industry. Strong connections between the manufacturing regions existed and, following the introduction of the railways, many businesses ran operations in both London and Luton.

Manufacturing processes

In order to turn straw plait into a hat, the plait must be sewn in a continuous coil, starting at the crown and ending at the brim. At first done by hand, sewers spent several years as apprentices perfecting tiny stitches that would be almost invisible in the finished item, and learning how to make a hat of the required size and shape. Most of this sewing was done in the home or in small establishments before being sold on to the larger firms.

The first known instance of sewing straw plaits by machine has been attributed to a Mrs Stratford who successfully used a Singer sewing machine for the task in 1874. This led to the introduction, by Willcox & Gibbs in 1875, of the Visible Stitch Machine, commonly known as the '10-guinea' machine due to its price, but the visibility of the stitches meant it was only suitable for coarser plaits.

In 1878, however, a Luton-based engineer by the name of Edmund Wiseman invented a reasonably priced concealed-stitch sewing machine that transformed the industry (Fig 23). Although it took around four years to train a girl how to use a sewing machine on all types of hat, she was then able to sew six hats in the time it would have taken her to sew one by hand. Willcox & Gibbs acquired the design rights of the machine in 1886 and they soon became

Gas-heated hat blocks at the Barford Brothers Ltd's site on North Street, Luton. Although the industry is much reduced from its peak, Luton hat manufacturers still produce thousands of hats a year and the techniques remain largely unchanged.
[DP110708]

Figure 23
Edmund Wiseman, creator of the concealed-stitch sewing machine, poses with one of his creations at his workshop in 1907. His work revolutionised the industry and allowed manufacturers to mass-produce hats on a scale previously unseen.
[Luton Culture/The Luton News]

known as 'box machines' due to their distinctive shape. Many of these original machines, and a number of later versions, are still maintained and used today.

After sewing, the roughly shaped hats would be blocked into their final shape using many of the processes that are still common practice today. At first the blocking was done by hand using smooth stones or box irons heated in a fire. In the hand-blocking process a hat is wetted or steamed and then quickly drawn over the crown of a block and pulled evenly on all sides before it dries. Machine blocking, introduced to the industry in *c* 1860, was done using screw presses until the invention of the application of hydraulic pressure around 1868. Each hat is placed in a metal pan of the required shape within a steam-heated chamber; a water-filled rubber bag is then lowered and by exerting equal pressure is capable of quickly shaping the hat against the pan. A popular alternative is to heat 'male' and 'female' blocks using a gas flame and, having first steamed the hat, simply press the two together. Blocking has historically tended to be done by male workers (Fig 24), due in part to the relatively late adoption of mechanisation, long after women had come to dominate as plaiters and sewers.

Hats can be dyed at various points in the hatting process – sometimes as straws or plait, and sometimes as sewn hats, or even both. Until the 1850s hat manufacturers tended to dye their own products but the range of colours available to them was limited. After the hats have been sewn, dyed

Figure 24
Men machine blocking straw boaters in a Luton hat factory, c *1907. Rows of roughly shaped hats can be seen hanging from the ceiling and to the side of the room, with a pile of finished hats in the centre ready to be sent for trimming.*
[Luton Culture/The Luton News]

and blocked, they are often immersed in a stiffening agent such as shellac or gelatine before being left to dry.

The final stage in the hatting process is to finish and trim the hats, the simplest level of finishing being the insertion of a lining and band since most trimming of women's hats was done by the in-house milliners of retailers. Over the course of the early 20th century, however, the 'half-millinery' trade was increasingly adopted where basic ribbons and bows are added, and this continued to develop until hat manufacturers were undertaking the complete finishing and trimming of the hats prior to them being sent to the retailers (Figs 25 and 26).

The manufacture of wool-felt hats is somewhat different in the initial stages, the raw wool being cleaned and carded to form a web which is then wound around a cone to form a hollow roll of 'cotton wool' – this process was, historically, almost always done by women as the fine web would catch on any hairs on the arms or hands and rip (Fig 27). The wool is then cut into individual pieces and steamed to create loosely felted 'forms'. Further

Figure 25 (above left)
Ribbons being dyed at the Barford Brothers' dye works on North Street, Luton. The process for dyeing straw, material, felt and feathers is much the same and is always done by hand.
[DP110686]

Figure 26 (above right)
Women at work in the trimmings section of the hat factory of Marida Ltd, Luton, in 1963. Trimming has always been carried out by hand and originally consisted of little more than a lining and a band, any other adornments being added by the milliner or retailer.
[Luton Culture/The Luton News]

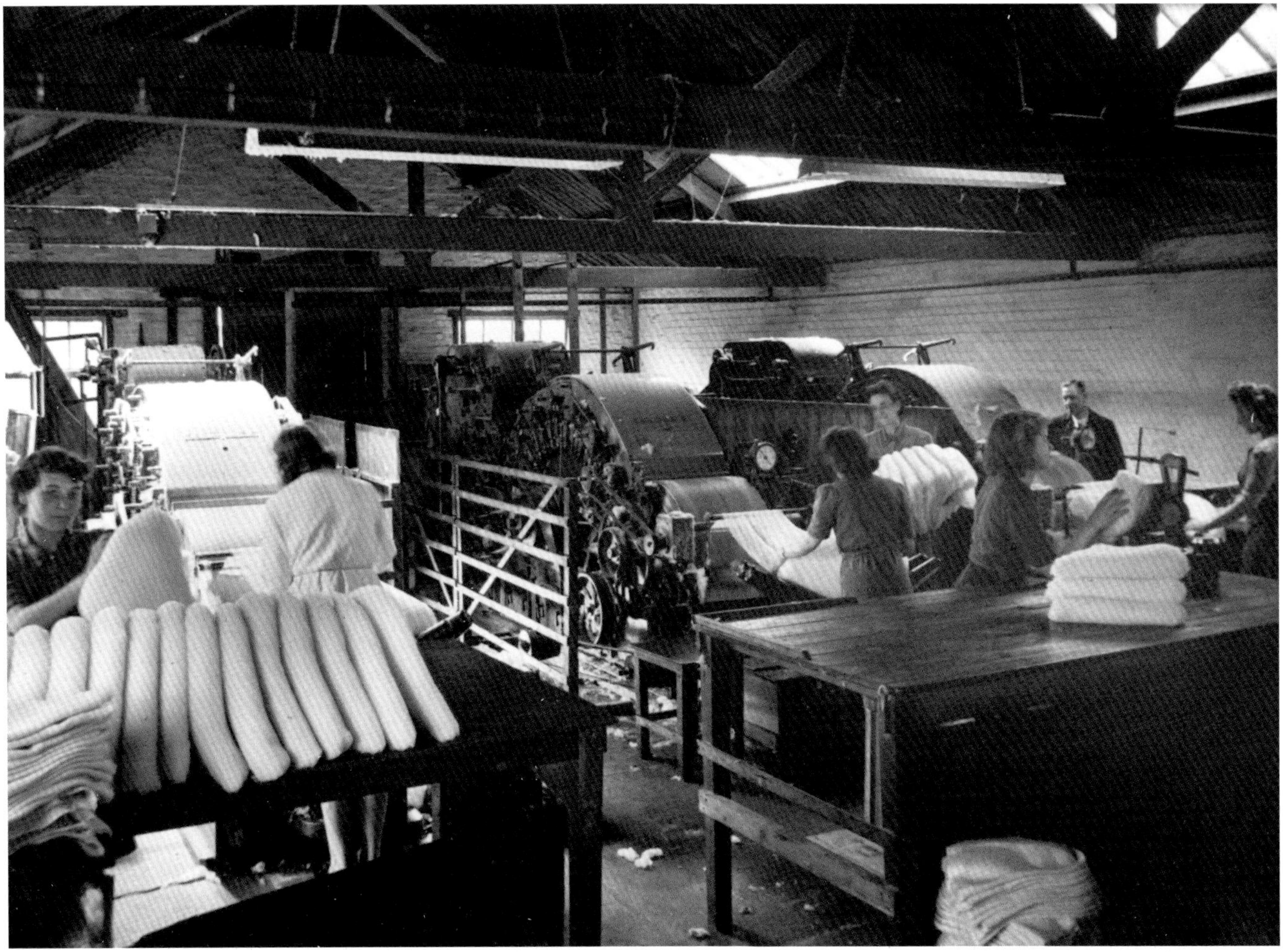

Figure 27
Women making cotton wool using carding machines in the Barford Brothers' dye works, c 1940. Wool felt was partly introduced in an attempt to spread work more evenly throughout the year, wool being a less seasonal product than straw.
[DP110772 courtesy of Mr John Horn]

steaming, rolling and pressing continues the felting process and involves comparatively heavy manual labour – these 'wet processes' are traditionally almost invariably carried out by men (Fig 28). At this point the form has been much reduced in size and is conical in shape, becoming known as a 'body'. Dyeing takes place at this stage before the body is steamed and stretched on a block to open out the crown and create a less conical, more recognisably hat-shaped, 'hood'. The blocking of the hoods is very painful to do and blockers quickly develop large calluses from the heat and roughness of the felt. At this stage of production some of the crudely shaped hoods might be sold to the millinery industry where they are known as 'capelines'. The method

of production from there onwards is very much the same as in straw-hat manufacture – after being steamed the hoods are blocked into shape, stiffened if required and left to dry before being lined and trimmed.

The processes involved in manufacturing fur-felt hats, prevalent in the north of England, were quite different in the initial stages and involved much greater risk to the workers. Although beaver fur was used for high-end hats, most of the fur for mass production came from rabbits which were prepared by furriers who first graded the pelts by quality before flattening them, removing the tail and legs. The pelts were then cured using a mixture of acid and mercury – the toxic mercuric nitrate, when inhaled over a prolonged period

Figure 28
Men tended to undertake the heavier processes, including the rolling and pressing of felt as seen here in the Barford Brothers' dye works, c 1940, where a Mazzera multi-roller is being used.
[DP110766 courtesy of Mr John Horn]

of time, often resulted in mercury poisoning. The early symptoms included shaking, slurring and forgetfulness, leading eventually to confusion, mental distress and death – hence the term 'mad as a hatter'. Although workers were afforded greater protective equipment when dealing with mercury from 1899 onwards, it continued to be used in large quantities until 1939. (The workers in the Luton hat industry were fortunate not to be exposed to such dangers.) After curing, the coarse outer hairs were removed from the pelts before the soft fur was separated from the skin. The fur would then be prepared for felting by bowing, or later blowing, the fur – processes whereby the fur was fluffed up with moving air, ensuring that any remaining coarse fur or hair would fall away whilst the fine, soft, fur would be gathered together ready for use. The process thereafter was not dissimilar to that of wool-felt manufacture – if done by hand a hatter would shape the fur into triangles, inserting a triangular slip of cloth or paper between two to stop them matting together in the middle, before pressing and rolling the fur triangles to make the edges mat together and create a hood. Thomas Christy, of Christy & Co Hatters, introduced fur-felting machines to England in 1859 whereby fur was adhered to a revolving cone and loosely felted using hot water. The hoods were then boiled or steamed, rollered, shaped and blocked in the same way as wool-felt hats before being 'pounced', or sandpapered, to align the hairs before being 'lured' using animal fat, wire or sharkskin to achieve the desired smooth, furry or 'peach bloom' finish.

Economy and organisation

The imposition of punitive import tariffs during the Napoleonic Wars ensured a firm economic basis for the domestic production of straw hats using local plait. By the time tariffs were relaxed in the peacetime years immediately after 1815, business around Luton was already well established and able to withstand the resumption of foreign competition. Tariffs were finally removed altogether in 1842 but, rather than dampening the growth of the industry, this was followed by further expansion and specialisation.

One of the main reasons for the success and rapid expansion of the hatting industry was the relatively low set-up costs for new businesses and the high returns that might reasonably be expected. For instance, in 1860 1 shilling's worth of straw could be transformed into between £7 13s and £15 of finished goods – a return of between 15,000 per cent and 30,000 per cent, less labour and production costs.

Hat manufacturing received a further boost when the local plait trade collapsed at the end of the 19th century, with plaiters forced to turn their hands to the sewing and finishing of hats. Subsequently, Luton expanded faster than almost any other place in southern England (Fig 29) – in 1821 it was a small town with a population of 2,986 but by 1861 it had more than 15,000 residents. Similar patterns of growth were seen in other towns and villages in the area. Dunstable, for example, grew from a population of 1,296 in 1801 to 5,157 in 1901, whilst the village of Markyate went from a total of 105 in 1841 to 317 in 1901.

The increased mechanisation witnessed within the hatting industry, particularly in the last quarter of the 19th century, was at first expected to put an end to homeworking and small firms. The machines, however, were available to hire or buy relatively cheaply. Blocking benches and irons could be operated just as well at home as in a factory and thus actually enabled the smaller manufacturers to compete better with the larger firms. Before the introduction of wool-felt hatting to Luton it was possible to start up a new business with as little as £5 – sewing machines could be hired, whilst blocking benches and irons could all be accommodated within a domestic scullery.

The felt-hat industry, which supplanted the straw-hat industry, was a late arrival to the region, despite felting being the older and more important trade in most other areas of England. It was introduced in the 1870s in an attempt to provide a steady source of work less reliant on the seasonal harvest and its by-product of straw. The manufacture of felt hats greatly expanded after the First World War, with felt rapidly replacing straw as the fashionable material of choice. By 1939 it accounted for more than 75 per cent of the Luton hat trade – unsurprising, perhaps, when it is considered that men of all social classes were expected to wear a hat at all times, even to attend a football match or go to work in a factory. The introduction of wool-felt saw start-up costs increase to around £200 to cover the purchase of a boiler, blocking machine and several sewing machines – which, although still very reasonable compared to many industries, was a more considerable investment. If firms wanted to create their

Figure 29
The Easter bonnet parade on George Street, Luton, in 1955. This annual event celebrated the industry and tens of thousands of workers from across the region would take part in the processions, floats and competitions throughout the day.
[Luton Culture/The Luton News]

own hoods they needed to buy at least 10 forming machines at a cost of around £1,700 to £2,500, and employ between 40 and 60 workers to make a viable business.

The hat industry was divided up into firms which were classed as 'manufacturers', 'makers-up', 'wholesalers', or 'direct traders' according to their methods of production and sale. Manufacturers occupied the large warehouses and factories in the centre of Luton, St Albans and Dunstable. In 1935 there were seven such factories in Luton employing 1,000 women and 900 men between them, with the largest firms of Munt & Brown, Vyse, and Elliott employing as many as 500 workers each, whereas the smallest had only around 100 workers. The makers-up, or makers, carried out the same work as the manufacturers but in small, largely domestic units, and sold their goods to the wholesalers or factories – a hangover from the days of plaiting. In 1939 there were at least 125 makers in Luton, the largest of whom employed around 100 workers, whilst the smallest made do with just 5 or 6 (Fig 30). Many manufacturers also employed homeworkers (Fig 31), who worked in a similar manner, and it has been estimated that the domestic-scale industry accounted for more than three-quarters of all the straw hats made in and around Luton. This has had a significant impact on the design of houses in the area.

The manufacturing branches of wholesalers tended to use their Luton factories for mass production work, retaining their London factories for finer work. The largest of these employed 400 workers in Luton, the smallest, fewer than 50. The final branch of the industry, direct traders, manufactured their own goods and dealt directly with retailers. This business model emerged *c* 1920 and by 1939 there were around 20 such traders, the largest employing about 350 people, and few employing under 100 workers.

Many firms were family owned and one particular family, the Wallers, were particularly influential in establishing Luton as a town of industry. A prominent local family of hat manufacturers, they played an important role in bringing the railway to the town and were ruthless in developing their business interests, buying up land in the centre of Luton whenever the opportunity arose. The best known of the Waller family were two brothers, Edmund and Thomas. Thomas concentrated on the buying and selling of plaits, at first buying plait from the prisoners of war at Yaxley Barracks, near Peterborough, before he successfully patented the use of Italian straws to create 'Tuscan

Figure 30 (above left)
The staff of the Reginald Hat Manufacturing Company Ltd pose outside the factory in 1950. The organisation of the industry meant than there were many smaller factories, employing perhaps 20 to 30 workers, who sold their goods on to larger factories or dealers.
[Luton Culture/The Luton News]

Figure 31 (above right)
A homeworker on her way to deliver a completed order to a Luton factory in 1950. Most of the factories employed as many homeworkers as they did regular employees.
[Luton Culture/The Luton News]

Straw Bonnets' in 1826, the first successful rival to the highly fashionable but expensive and hard to obtain Leghorn straw hats. One contemporary remarked that 'he was of very quick perception, and equally prompt in decision. When his judgement was once formed it was not easily changed.'[5]

Edmund Waller was a straw-hat manufacturer but also established a warehouse in the centre of Luton which allowed him to buy large numbers of hats from domestic workers in the area, helping to establish the later counter trade whereby individual makers-up would sell their work on to the larger factories. Along with other individuals, such as Corston and Lancaster who experimented with different types of grass and rye, his efforts helped to encourage new firms to set up their factories in Luton – including Welch, Willis and Elliott, as well as Munt & Brown.

Subsidiary industries

Hat manufacturing relied upon a number of specialised ancillary industries such as box making, bleaching and dyeing, gelatine production, and blockmaking – these trades tended to employ far more men than plaiting or sewing but also worked on a relatively small scale, the largest blockmakers employing fewer than 40 men. Box manufacturers produced the large cardboard boxes which were used to transport the hats by train across the country, but this aspect of the trade gradually became absorbed by the larger factories following the introduction of wool-felt hats – it was a way to make use of wool scraps by incorporating the fibres into the boxes, thus maximising profits.

The earliest method of bleaching, first recorded in 1748, involved plaiters dampening bundles of straws and placing them into a sealed box containing burning sulphur. As the industry evolved so too did bleaching methods, culminating in companies which specialised in the use of hydrogen peroxide – a method of bleaching which had the added benefit of removing minor discolorations. Similarly, until the mid-19th century the dyeing of straws was done on a small scale using a limited range of natural dyes – such as the blue obtained from the damsons for which the Aylesbury region was famed. The first local dye works was established in Sundon in *c* 1845 by William Randall, but with the introduction of synthetic dyes the bleaching and dyeing industry expanded rapidly and in 1857 Thomas Lye set up as Luton's first independent dyer, leading the way for an increasingly important supporting industry (Fig 32).

Before the introduction of shellac, gelatine had commonly been used for the stiffening of straw hats and demand increased greatly through the 19th century. Accordingly, in 1903 the British Gelatine Works opened on Bedford Road, Luton, and although it largely produced gelatine for photographic usage, the requirements of the hat industry must have been considered when choosing the location. The works occupied more than 10 acres (4ha) before its eventual closure and redevelopment in 2002.

Blockmakers produced the wooden blocks and aluminium pans used to shape the hats to their desired forms. Early timber blocks were generally made from alder or lime and, whilst lime remains popular today, tulip and especially

Figure 32
Thomas Lye founded a dye and bleach works on Old Bedford Road, Luton, in 1857. This impressive site, with louvre-sided drying rooms clearly visible on the right, closed in the 1960s and the buildings were demolished in 1990.
[Luton Culture]

obeche are also used, as they have minimal imperfections and are soft yet durable enough to be pinned. Simple shapes are made from a single piece of timber, whereas more complicated designs might involve five or more sections. The downside of wooden blocks is that hats, dampened before blocking, are dried at room temperature which generally means that only a single hat can be blocked in a day. Metal hat pans, which are formed of a upper and lower section pressed together, are better suited to the demands of mass manufacture as the metal is heated and therefore simultaneously shapes and dries the hats, allowing as many as 300 or so to be blocked in a single day.

The manufacturing method for hat pans begins with the blocker carving a plaster version of the completed hat shape (Fig 33), sometimes working to a brief from a designer but often creating a design from scratch. This plaster hat is then used to create a packed-sand cast (Fig 34) into which molten aluminium (in the early years, iron or even zinc) is poured (Fig 35).

Figure 33
Boon & Lane Ltd of Taylor Street, Luton, carve plaster versions of the hat shapes they wish to create. The company manufacture the blocks and hat pans used by many high-profile clients, including international fashion designers, film makers and the royal family.
[DP153597]

Figure 34
Steve Lane, of Boon & Lane Ltd, creates a sand cast of a hat. This highly skilled trade is now almost extinct in the UK, Boon & Lane being the last surviving firm.
[DP153609]

Figure 35
Molten aluminium is poured into the cavity of a mould at Boon & Lane Ltd. A complicated hat shape might require five separate pieces, or even more, to be cast in order that they fit together in such a way as to allow the hat to be removed once it has been blocked.
[DP153657]

Working conditions

As the female-dominated industry developed during the late 19th century, a lack of male labour meant that unionisation in Luton was almost unheard of – as a result relatively low wages remained unchallenged, which only further encouraged firms to employ more women. In the largest factories there was an average of about 10 women to every man, and out of the 24 factories in Bedfordshire employing more than 50 workers there were only 183 men compared to 1,928 women.

Luton thus gained a reputation as a place where the men were kept by the women – the Luton Chamber of Commerce going so far, in 1900, as to produce a booklet aimed at attracting new industry to the town by advertising the advantage of being able to pay men at low rates since the female members of the family were already employed.[6]

Despite the fact that women undertook some of the most skilled work in the industry, rates of pay between the sexes varied greatly. The Hat, Cap and Millinery Trade Board was set up in 1919 to oversee the regulation of wages, both for fixed-rate workers and for those employed on a piecework basis. The suggested wages for workers in 1939 were 1s 5d an hour for skilled male labourers, 1s 1d for unskilled males and 7½d for female labourers. These figures, whilst well below what workers could actually expect to achieve, suggest that the industry worked on the basis of paying women approximately half of what men received – this only changed in 1944 when women's earnings were set at 68 per cent of men's.

It took about four years to train a girl to become sufficiently skilled to work with all types of plait (Fig 36). Much in demand, girls quickly found that the large factories of Luton or St Albans offered higher wages for shorter hours than they were used to in the smaller businesses around the town, and it was therefore unusual for a girl to stay with a small firm once her training was complete aged 18.

Many girls aspired to become a sewer in one of the urban hat factories, a sewer being 'considered a step above a plaiter, and one who may exhibit a certain amount of personal adornment, to which a simple plaiter would not dare aspire in her village home'.[7] The sewers in Luton and St Albans benefited from reasonably comfortable working conditions and hours, in some part due to the fact that plaiters had long been used to their independence and saw no reason why this should change because they were in a new role. Indeed, when factory inspectors visited Luton in 1867 they found that:

> The girls, accustomed to going to work when they pleased, dressed in nice clothes, resented being classed as factory workers who, they imagined, answered the dictates of a factory bell and went to work in clogs and a shawl. One girl complained to the Dunstable bench that a factory inspector had been rude to her: it seems that he had called her a 'straw-plait girl' and not 'young lady' in the manner to which she was accustomed.[8]

The production of straw, and therefore of straw hats, necessarily depended upon the seasons and, consequently, there was always more work to be had in the spring and early summer. Sewers or 'hands' were paid by piecework –

Figure 36
An apprenticeship agreement setting out the terms of employment for the 14-year-old Kathleen Ackroyd. She was taught the millinery trade by her mother, Mrs Alice Ackroyd, at the newly rebuilt Vyse, Sons and Co Ltd factory on Bute Street, Luton, and her pay increased as she became more skilled.
[Courtesy of the Ackroyd family]

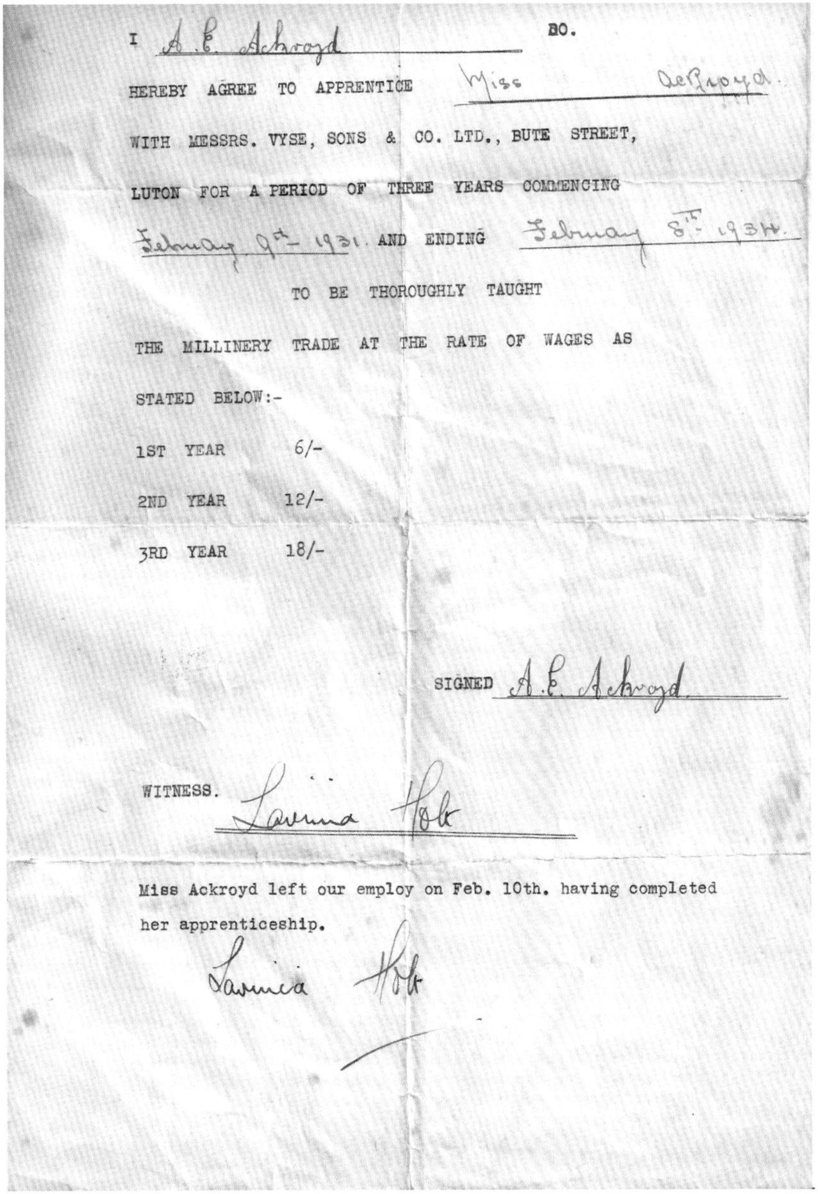

I A. E. Ackroyd DO.

HEREBY AGREE TO APPRENTICE Miss Ackroyd.

WITH MESSRS. VYSE, SONS & CO. LTD., BUTE STREET,

LUTON FOR A PERIOD OF THREE YEARS COMMENCING

February 9th – 1931. AND ENDING February 8th – 1934.

TO BE THOROUGHLY TAUGHT

THE MILLINERY TRADE AT THE RATE OF WAGES AS

STATED BELOW:-

1ST YEAR 6/-

2ND YEAR 12/-

3RD YEAR 18/-

SIGNED A. E. Ackroyd.

WITNESS. Lavinia Holt

Miss Ackroyd left our employ on Feb. 10th. having completed her apprenticeship.

Lavinia Holt

Figure 37
Firemen attempt to extinguish a fire at the premises of Ashton & Sons on Silver Street, Luton, in 1954. Fires were an all too common occurrence in hat factories, but thankfully rarely fatal.
[Luton Culture/The Luton News]

how many hats or bonnets they had sewn that week – and factory discipline was unknown, with the sewers working the hours that best suited them, often working through the night as they wanted to make as much money as they could whilst work was plentiful.

Conversely, those unfortunate enough to be employed within the London millinery trade (as opposed to hat manufacturing proper) often had to endure quite different working conditions. Girls entered millinery and dressmaking apprenticeships in London at the age of 14, generally for a period of two years. A Government report of 1843 revealed the horrific working conditions they endured. They worked for around 15 hours a day as standard, but were forced to work for up to 22 hours a day for months at a time if demand was high – one girl reported working for 78½ hours straight, with the exception of ½ an hour to sit and rest, following the death of William IV and the consequent increase in demand for black mourning caps. Often they would be too exhausted even to go home at the end of the day, indeed it was common for the girls to collapse in the workroom and sleep where they lay. One witness, Queen Victoria's personal physician, testified that:

> A mode of life more completely calculated to destroy human health could scarcely be contrived … And I have long been most anxious to see something done to rescue these unfortunate girls from the slavery to which they are subjected.[9]

Fire was a constant risk in the crowded semi-domestic factories of the suburbs, where the buildings were filled with flammable materials and gas-fired blocking machines. Outbreaks, however, were generally quickly discovered and rarely proved fatal. Fires in the multi-storey factories of the town centres were a far greater risk (Fig 37), and the best documented fire in Luton occurred at the Vyse factory on Bute Street in 1930. The subsequent enquiry, reported in *The Times*, found that shortly after noon on 25 February an employee dropped a pail of boiling beeswax in the basement and within minutes the whole building was ablaze.[10] The factory had not contained any fire extinguishing equipment and there was no external fire escape; most of the employees escaped but others were trapped on the third floor and, tragically, eight lost their lives.

5

Buildings of the hat industry

As with any trade, not all of the buildings used by the hat industry were purpose-built, and a few were shared with other businesses – several hat factories or warehouses occupied a floor or wing of a larger building, something seen particularly in Luton town centre where space was at a premium. However, where space and money allowed, new types of buildings designed specifically for the industry emerged. The organisation of the hat trade was particularly complex, with manufacturers, makers-up, wholesalers, dealers, merchants and direct traders all playing their part. The buildings of the industry reflected this complexity with different building types emerging to meet the needs of these groups, capable of providing a place of work for anything between one and 400 or more workers, as appropriate.

Small-scale industry

Plaiting was largely a domestic industry and, with the exception of the long demolished plait halls of Luton, Dunstable and Hitchin, very few buildings were purpose-built for the trade. Most plaiters worked in their own homes and there is now scant evidence for this, apart from documentary or local knowledge, since little architectural modification was required. A remarkable exception to this rule is a pair of small, unassuming two-storey outbuildings (Fig 38) in Edlesborough, Buckinghamshire, 8 miles to the west of Luton. These buildings of *c* 1880, with their matchboarded first-floor stores (Fig 39) over a workshop, belonged to a straw-plait dealer and dyer by the name of Ezra Janes who had a copper still on the ground floor of one in which he reportedly boiled up damsons to create an allegedly popular dye.

Otherwise, one physical clue which may hint at a building having been occupied and used by a straw plaiter is a series of notches in the beam above a fireplace. It is said that plaiters would often incise a series of notches at one quarter, one half and one full yard intervals in order to have a convenient and fast way to measure their work. However, evidence for this practice is lacking – possibly because the marks are easily overlooked or obscured by later alterations.

Many smaller properties in Luton and the surrounding towns and villages were designed with the requirements of the hat industry in mind – from

Decorative stone and brickwork around a window at the former Walter Gurney & Son Ltd hat factory, 64 Bute Street, Luton, built in 1889.

subtle changes to a house where some sewing or blocking might occur, right through to houses which were entirely designed for use by the industry. All of these buildings tended to be built with a basement, a passage to the rear, and sometimes a 'straw-gate' which allowed cart access to the rear of the property where the rear wing might be considerably larger than in a purely domestic property.

Terence Paul Smith, an industrial archaeologist, identified three major house plans specific to the industry in the region (Fig 40), increasing in complexity throughout the late 19th century and into the early 20th century.[11] Although variations and anomalies exist, the typology is a useful indicator as to the date and function of buildings in the region. Type one was essentially a standard terraced house of *c* 1860–70 and consisted of a front room and living room divided by stairs which ran parallel to the street, with two bedrooms above. The front door opened directly into the front room, and the rear wing was half the width of the main house. This rear wing contained a kitchen accessed directly from the living room with an exterior door into the yard, from where the coal-house and WC were accessed. For the purposes of the hat industry, however, the kitchen doubled as a workshop for the heavy processes

Figure 38 (above left)
A pair of outbuildings to the rear of a house in Edlesborough which was used by a straw plait dealer and dyer at the end of the 19th century. Similar in scale to outbuildings designed for use by the boot and shoe industry in Long Buckby, Northamptonshire, these examples were constructed around 10 years earlier and the internal arrangement of workshop and storage area appears to be reversed.
[DP154569]

Figure 39 (above right)
These outbuildings consisted of a first-floor store which was boarded to prevent the plait from becoming damp, with a taking-in door for the easy transfer of the plait. The ground-floor workroom was connected to the store by a ladder stair.
[DP154575]

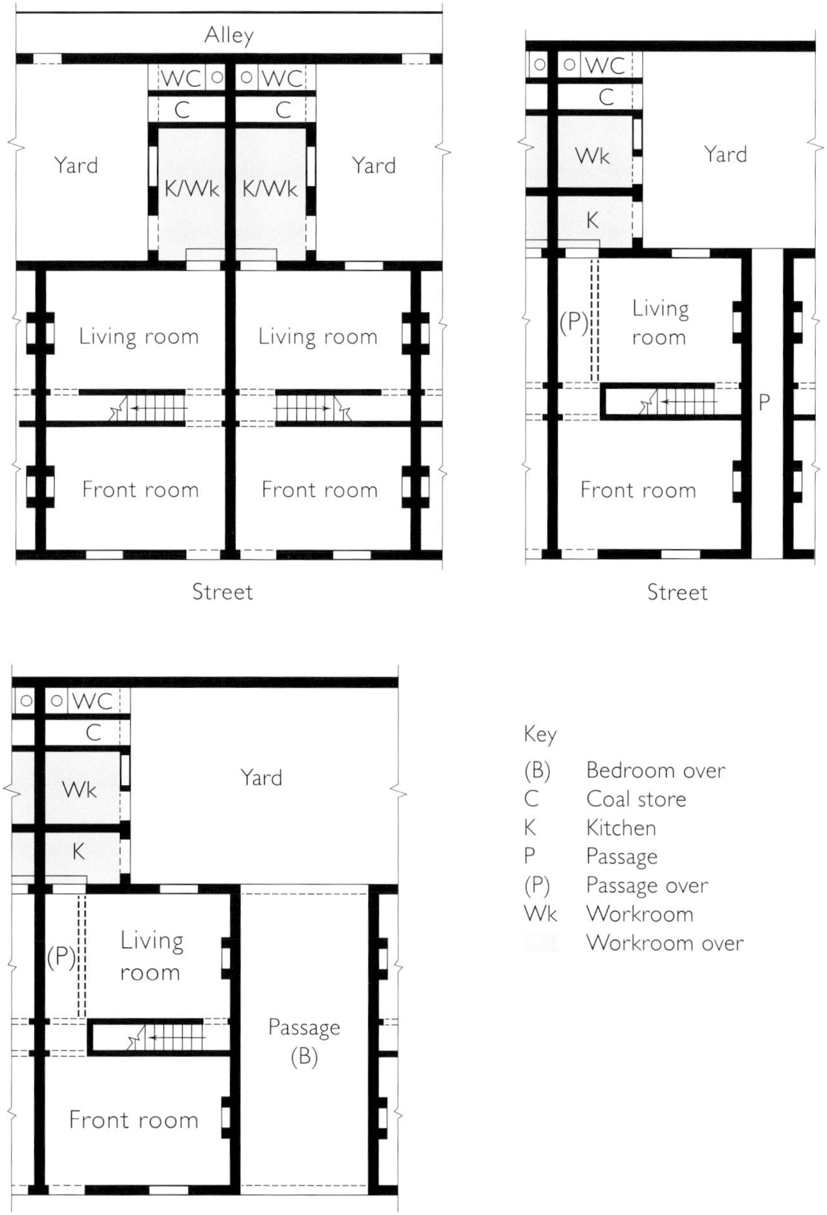

Figure 40
House plans associated with the hat industry: type one, c 1860–70 (top left); type two, c 1870–1900 (top right); type three, c 1900–14 (bottom).

of blocking and stiffening, which required a water supply. Above, a room which was accessed directly from the rear bedroom was used for sewing and storage – often proving too small for habitation as a bedroom. The houses backed on to an alley which could be accessed from the yard.

Type two is more clearly specialised for use by the industry and is slightly later in date, generally being constructed between *c* 1870 and 1900. These houses were built in pairs with a narrow passageway between every other house allowing pedestrian access from the road into the yard to the rear. The front of the house remained the same as in type one, but the rear wing contained a smaller kitchen which was divided from the workroom beyond by a wall, and the workroom itself was accessed from the yard rather than directly off the kitchen. The upper workroom could be accessed internally by a passageway, or externally by means of a separate staircase, but there was no direct access from the lower workroom to the upper.

Type three, prevalent *c* 1900–14, was essentially the same as type two but with a wider passageway to allow vehicular access, often via double gates in the street frontage (Figs 41, 42 and 43). The wider passageway also allowed for a third bedroom above.

These buildings can often appear entirely domestic when viewed from the street (Figs 44 and 45), and indeed are often surrounded by solely residential dwellings – sometimes it is only when the back of the property is visible that it becomes obvious that the rear wing is too large for a purely domestic house (Figs 46, 47 and 48). The first-floor workshops required a large amount of light and generally had very large windows, often with industrial-style metal frames rather than standard domestic sashes (Fig 49). The very largest of these semi-domestic properties in Luton date to around 1905–10 and are found in the High Town area to the north, and Hazelbury Crescent to the west, of the town centre. It is noticeable that by far the majority of these buildings were built with their workshops facing south. This appears to indicate a level of environmental determinism whereby the requirement of the industry and the need for natural light were considered when these new roads were being laid out – the north side of the street being largely reserved for purely residential buildings and the south side for light industry.

Given the extent to which the industry relied upon small-scale manufacture and homeworking, remarkably few of these buildings survive

Figure 41 (opposite)
These reasonably unassuming buildings on Buxton Road, Luton, are examples of small-scale semi-domestic premises. The 1914 Luton Year Book and Directory *describes 71, with its paired blue-painted doors, as the premises of the hat manufacturer A Healey. 73, with its cart entrance, was used by another hat manufacturer by the name of Stygall & Grundy. Extra entrances are often a good indication as to a possible commercial or industrial function in otherwise domestic looking buildings. [DP153983]*

Figure 42 (above right)
Many of Luton's suburbs contain small-scale hat factories. The area around Stanley Street, to the south of the town centre, is characterised by tall, terraced properties – many with integrated cartways known locally as 'straw gates'. [DP153885]

Figure 43 (right)
Some of these small-scale factories attempted to stand out from their competitors by virtue of size or design. 81 Dumfries Street, Luton, is notably larger than its immediate neighbours and also displays rather more in the way of architectural embellishment; red-brick detailing contrasting with the plum colour of the Luton stock bricks. [DP154580]

outside of Luton's suburbs. A few examples may still be found in Dunstable and St Albans, but the vast majority have disappeared. The largest concentrations can be found in the High Town area of Luton, and in the area around Princess Street, to the south of the town centre.

Dunstable's manufacturers did not rely on outworkers in the same way as the Luton companies did, and there are proportionally far fewer domestic-scale examples of workshops to be found in the town. This may in part be due to the fact that many Dunstable firms, such as Munt & Brown, who occupied the Priory and the adjacent, long-demolished, factory also had factories in Luton and chose to concentrate their workforce in the one place.

The few domestic-scale workshops that existed were centred on Edward Street and a number have been listed at Grade II in recognition of their

Figure 44 (above left)
Some properties, such as 84 Princess Street, Luton, invested in detailing and a quality of design which went beyond the utilitarian.
[DP153986]

Figure 45 (above right)
Premises designed for use by the hat industry can often be readily identified by the size of their rear wings. As with 69 Havelock Road, Luton, even when a building appears identical to its neighbours when seen from the front, the rear wing is considerably longer than would be expected in a purely domestic property.
[DP154615]

Figure 46 (above)
A view of the back of houses on Clarendon Road, Luton, in c 1921 showing the characteristically long rear ranges of domestic-scale hat factories. This road has changed very little in the intervening years and is still home to a number of working hat factories and other businesses associated with the trade.
[Luton Culture/The Luton News]

Figure 47 (above right)
The rear ranges were well-lit spaces with independent access from the yard they faced, sometimes at first floor as well as ground floor – as with these hat factories on Reginald Street, Luton.
[DP154614]

Figure 48 (right)
Sometimes the extensions to the rear of the houses were a little more piecemeal in development, with a series of extensions to the original workshop a common sight as businesses expanded.
[DP154622]

architectural merit, although their role in the hat industry does not appear to have been acknowledged. Surrounded by a large number of non-designated hat factories, these buildings are distinguished from the houses around them by their greater architectural embellishment. The earlier examples make use of fine-gauged red-brick detailing to the façade (Fig 50), whilst the slightly later buildings have bracketed consoles at the windows and eaves, often used in conjunction with a striking triple window arrangement on the first floor (Fig 51).

The ease with which buildings could be adapted for use for the hat industry, and the reasonably low cost of building more specialised premises, meant that the industry could spread out to the smaller towns and villages of the region. One example of this was Markyate, along Watling Street to the south-west of Luton, which had served the needs of long-distance travellers since the introduction of stagecoaches in the 1650s. However, by the 1830s the railways had diverted most of the trade away and the town turned instead to the hatting industry for its survival. Unusually, it focused on manufacturing rather than plaiting and therefore had more in common with larger urban centres such as Luton or Dunstable than with outlying villages such as Kensworth and Studham, where plaiting dominated.

The 1861 census, averaged across the parishes that formed Markyate, shows that 60 per cent of all the houses were home to one or more people working in the hatting industry, with over 30 per cent of all the town's

Figure 49 (above left)
The workshops were often lit by large, metal-framed windows and were simply constructed with minimal architectural or artistic design. This created buildings with a pleasingly industrial aesthetic when seen from the rear, at odds with the domestic appearance when viewed from the street.
[DP154621]

Figure 50 (above right)
31 Edward Street, Dunstable. This fine building was erected in c 1850 and in the 1870s it was home to a stonemason and his children, two of whom were straw-bonnet sewers.
[DP154584]

residents (including children) directly involved. Streets such as Albert Street, which was built as New Street in the late 1850s, demonstrate how the town had rapidly adapted to meet the requirements of the industry – 11 out of the 12 houses on this street were home to one or more people working in the industry, with at least five of the houses being a workplace as well as a residence. Peter Lacey, for example, ran a hat factory from his home at 9 Albert Street (Fig 52), and the workshops and rear ranges behind the house are still just visible today (Fig 53).

Large numbers of horses were employed in the transportation of hats and materials. Many stables are shown on maps of the 19th century, but very few of those related to the industry have survived. One still stands in Luton town

Figure 51 (above)
33 Edward Street, Dunstable. The Italianate detailing suggests that this building was constructed in c 1870, and by 1871 it was home to Naomi Gurney, a straw-bonnet sewer, and her two young children.
[DP154585]

Figure 52 (right)
Domestic-scale hat factories may still be found outside of Luton but they are less densely concentrated and tend to be less well documented. One exception is 9 Albert Street, Markyate, which was home to Peter Lacey's hat factory.
[DP153742]

centre at the rear of 43 Guildford Street (Fig 54), formerly a domestic-scale hat factory. Further out, another stable survives on William Street in the High Town area of Luton. A single-storey building, it was erected in 1911 to house the horses belonging to the Barford Brothers' dye and bleach works on North Street.

Figure 53 (above left)
*The rear wing of Lacey's factory (*see *Fig 52) was, over time, connected to a previously free-standing workshop where heavier processes such as blocking were carried out.*
[DP153743]

Figure 54 (above right)
A rare survivor – a stable in central Luton. Horses were once crucial to the industry as they pulled the carts loaded with boxes of hats to and from the railway stations, from where the hats would be taken by special trains to London.
[DP141928]

Large-scale industry

In the urban centres of Luton, St Albans and Dunstable, buildings of a more commercial nature can be found. The earliest of the factories and warehouses were brick-built and employed traditional building methods, but they were far larger and more clearly commercial in design (Figs 55, 56, 57 and 58).

With the development of cast-iron, steel and concrete construction methods in the late 19th and early 20th centuries, however, the way was paved for a far more obviously industrial aesthetic than previously seen. Although still on a small scale to begin with, the use of cast iron and, later, steel and concrete allowed for large, uninterrupted spaces lit by large banks of windows (Figs 59, 60, 61 and 62). As a result the scale and complexity of the industrial premises increased dramatically, culminating in the emergence of 'daylight' factories – large, flat-roofed buildings with a steel or concrete frame dominated by the provision of glazing (Figs 63 and 64).

These buildings demonstrate one of the key developments in the late 19th-century industry, the emergence of a characteristic plan form readily identifiable as a hat factory or warehouse. The diagnostic features include a raised ground-floor wholesale showroom with a display window and recessed lobby above a basement, often with a second entrance to the side of the building (Fig 65).

Figure 55 (above)
47 Guildford Street – the earliest known hat factory in central Luton was built in c 1840 and is still largely domestic in appearance. It was built using traditional building materials and methods, with Luton grey bricks, stuccoed detailing and sash windows.
[DP146079]

Figure 56 (right)
Some premises sit uncomfortably between domestic and industrial designs. Whilst still apparently domestic when viewed from the street one such example, on Lemsford Road, St Albans, takes the concept of a rear-wing workshop to the extreme in terms of scale.
[DP153581]

Figure 57 (above left)
Some early factories favoured an alternative design where space allowed, constructing the factory element to the side of the house as here on Station Road, Ampthill. This had the advantage of clearly separating the two elements and allowing for easy access to the factory.
[DP153997]

Figure 58 (above right)
Even extensive warehouses or factories, such as those on Lower Dagnall Street, St Albans, might be designed in such a way as to almost mask the industrial or commercial nature of the property.
[DP153582]

Figure 59 (left)
In contrast to the properties on Lower Dagnall Street (see Fig 58), the former hat factory on Inkerman Road in St Albans is clearly industrial in nature. Although very similar in size and plan, the two buildings have been treated quite differently.
[DP153586]

Figure 60 (right)
Another clearly industrial warehouse at 2 George Street West, Luton. The emerging industrial aesthetic was largely made possible by the adoption of modern construction materials and techniques including steel frames and concrete floors.
[DP154589]

Figure 61 (below)
25 Wellington Street, Luton, is an unusual warehouse design with first- and second-floor showrooms as well as those on the ground floor, made possible by use of modern construction methods. Built in 1906 it is taller than surrounding buildings, framed by the buildings on Peel Street, its central position, height and symmetrical façade maximise its visual impact. Along with 21–23 it formed the hat warehouse and stores of J J Webdale & Sons, with further buildings extending to the rear of 27.
[DP154598]

Figure 62
This complex of buildings in Luton stretching from Dudley Street back to Albion Road and once all owned by Walter Wright Ltd demonstrates how changing construction methods and fashions affected the design of factory buildings. The earlier brick building at the back fronts Albion Road and is still home to Walter Wright Ltd, whilst the later steel-framed extension to the factory fronts Dudley Street.
[DP154608]

Figure 63
J & K Connor Ltd's hat factory on Bute Street, Luton, was built in 1927 and has a strongly industrial aesthetic, with long banks of windows and large, open floors marking it out as a 'daylight' factory. In 2003 it reopened as a council-owned and run arts and entertainment venue known as 'The Hat Factory'.
[DP141915]

Figure 64 (right)
The Connor hat factory under construction, as photographed by Bedford Lemere & Co on 22 February 1927. The steel frame around which the factory was built is clearly visible.
[BL28799_001]

Figure 65 (below)
16 John Street, Luton. Built in c 1880–90 this factory displays the characteristic plan form of raised ground-floor showroom with a display window and recessed lobby above a basement, with a second entrance to the side which allowed workers direct access to the rear of the property.
[DP146086]

Both factories and warehouses had ground-floor wholesale showrooms – simply furnished spaces which were designed to be functional rather than lavish display forums. Natural light from above was a favoured option whenever possible as it showed off the hats to their best advantage and a number of firms, where space allowed, built single-storey showroom extensions to the rear of the factories which allowed them to make use of skylights and ridge lanterns (Fig 66).

The provision of a passageway became increasingly widespread throughout the late 19th century as businesses expanded. The passageway not only allowed workers direct access to the rear of the building, but also access to a second lobby tucked away behind the main showroom. This lobby, or 'agents counter', was used by outworkers and others coming to sell their goods, rather than those individuals who came to purchase goods, who were welcomed by the main entrance and showroom.

Basements provided storage space for plait or packaged hats which could be loaded or unloaded directly from the street by means of the opening lights that ran beneath the raised ground-floor windows of the showroom or warehouse. Although in early examples the upper floors were occasionally still domestic, more often they were designed as well-lit workrooms and storage

Figure 66
The interior of a detached, single-storey, showroom which once stood to the rear of the Stevens & Gee Ltd factory on King Street, Luton. This simply laid out room was typical of many showrooms designed for display to commercial buyers rather than the public. It focused on the provision of natural light and allowed all the available designs to be viewed quickly and easily, with little in the way of additional decoration to distract the buyer.
[Luton Culture]

Figure 67
59 High Street South, Dunstable, was built in c *1860 and owned by the firm Munt & Brown. It was leased first to George Horn, a plait dealer, and then to Miss Eliza Osborne for use as a hat factory and the top floor was partitioned into seven small workrooms. The partially filled-in cart entrance and the large windows on the floors above suggest it was probably constructed with the requirements of the industry in mind.*
[DP153991]

spaces. This basic form would come to characterise the hat factories and warehouses of every period and style in the region.

However, the larger factories on Dunstable's High Street (Figs 67, 68, 69 and 70) are more domestic in appearance and less readily identifiable as hat factories than their Luton counterparts. Generally earlier than the factories of Luton or St Albans, these relatively plain buildings do not make use of raised ground-floor showrooms, and there are few examples with shopfronts or display windows, suggesting that the emphasis was on production of goods for a known buyer rather than public sales.

Many companies separated the dirtier processes, such as bleaching, dyeing, forming or blocking, from the finer ones of sewing and trimming. Where finances allowed, the preferred option was to have two premises – the factory tending to be a functional building on the outskirts of the town, with

greater investment evident in the central warehouses and showrooms. One example of this is the Barford Brothers' dye and bleach works on North Street in the High Town area of Luton (Fig 71). Purpose-built in 1894 by Gilbert and Ernest Barford, it specialised in the dyeing and bleaching of hats until it became part of a larger company by the 1950s. The site consists of a number of amalgamated buildings and, with the exception of the drying rooms, shows little in the way of architectural innovation. The drying rooms, however, are an exceptional survival – designed for drying out plait or hats after dyeing, the rooms have louvred wooden walls designed to encourage airflow (Fig 72). Such rooms would once have been a reasonably common sight in the region and there were a number of dedicated dye works, most of which also made use of drying yards where plait or hats could be left out to dry in the sun.

For most businesses, however, the division between the functions of factories and warehouses had become blurred by the second half of the 19th century. Both business models involved the production, buying and selling of hats and their component parts and this was reflected in the architecture of the industry. Rather than neatly separating manufacturing and warehousing by using

Figure 68 (above left)
48 High Street North, Dunstable. Built in 1851 this property is the first known purpose-built hat factory in Dunstable, the design based on a conventional late Georgian house. The factory was run until the late 1890s by the Waterfield family who, at one point, submitted a planning application for bay windows. The proposal caused uproar in the town with many people believing that such windows infringed public rights and would be unseemly, and the application was rejected.
[DP153989]

Figure 69 (above right)
15–17 High Street North, Dunstable. The present building was formed by the amalgamation of two separate businesses – that of William Oliver at 17, and of Benjamin Bennett at 15. Bennett bought Oliver's factory in around 1928 and knocked through dividing interior walls to create a new, larger, factory. As early as 1850 17, originally an 18th-century house, was described as a 10-bedroomed house with plait and workrooms, blocking house, two steam houses, bleach house, stable and a drying ground for plait.
[DP153993]

Figure 70
Similar in design to Waterfield's hat factory (see Fig 68), 36–40 High Street North was built by James Blackwell, a successful hat manufacturer, and leased to the London-based firm Woolley Sanders & Co between c 1858 and 1927. Over the course of those 60 years the section of the building on the right, which may well have been built as a private house for Mr Blackwell, was home to a succession of five managers.
[DP153987]

Figure 71
The Barford Brothers' dye works on North Street, Luton. The simple buildings of this purpose-built complex, still in use as a dye works today, although at a much reduced scale, generally display little in the way of architectural pretension or innovation, but provided the large, open spaces required by the industry.
[DP154607]

Figure 72
A louvre-sided drying room at Barford Brothers Ltd's site – a rare example of a once common feature across the region. The wooden sides of such rooms allowed for the maximum flow of air through the rooms, helping to speed up the drying process, whilst protecting the hats from damage.
[Katie Carmichael]

specialised premises, multifunctional premises were common and a building could easily be described and used as a factory one year and a warehouse the next. This was partly due to businesses altering their trade patterns to maximise the profits offered by rapid changes within the industry, but also to the fact that the owners of the buildings were rarely the occupiers and it was in their best interests to construct buildings which could be leased to different types of businesses and accommodate a variety of functions. Accordingly, flexibility of design which made use of well-lit open spaces was crucial.

The machinery used within the industry could be powered by gas, steam or electricity, with Munt & Brown's of Luton using steam-powered blocking machines as early as 1864, and Vyse using steam-powered sewing machines by 1881. Although gas had been introduced to Luton in 1834 it was considered too volatile to be fully embraced by manufacturers and it was the introduction of mains water in 1870 and electricity in 1900 that encouraged many to adopt

Figure 73
The Walter Gurney & Son Ltd hat factory on Bute Street, Luton. Built in 1889 it has a particularly complex façade with pink granite pilasters and stone detailing used in contrast with the red brick. Stone mullions, transoms, architraves, cartouches and swags are used to enrich the appearance of the building and impress visitors. [DP157637]

mechanisation. However, the increased adoption of mechanised production had a minimal impact on the design of the buildings, especially given that the machines were free-standing, generally quite small, and could be moved to new premises if required. The greatest impact was the weight of the machinery required for the production of felt hats. This necessitated reinforced floors – later factories tended to make use of pre-cast concrete, but timber floors strengthened by rolled steel joists (RSJs) remained common.

One of the most striking trends in the late 19th century years of expansion and development was towards increasing monumentality, ostentation and height expressed in the architecture of the industry. There was a prevalence, from the 1880s onwards, of four- and five-storey factory and warehouse blocks and the increased investment evident in the choice of architectural styles reflects not only the adoption of buildings of a suitably industrial scale to allow for mass production, but also increased confidence within the industry and a desire to impress visitors or passers-by through a display of prosperity.

As such, the newly constructed buildings displayed increasingly accomplished designs incorporating decorative motifs in immediate contrast with the simpler, and relatively unadorned, earlier buildings. All of the most visually impressive buildings front onto main thoroughfares and are eye-catching, intentionally so, with great emphasis on the treatment of façades.

The architects, builders and owners made full use of a variety of styles, including polychromy, Queen Anne Revival and neo-Jacobean. The Walter Gurney & Son Ltd hat factory at 64 Bute Street, Luton (Fig 73), the Durler & Suter hat factory at 50 Guildford Street, Luton (Fig 74), and Henry Durler & Son's hat factory and warehouse at 40 Guildford Street, Luton (Fig 75), epitomised this phase of confident expansion in the industry. Huge effort was expended in their design and construction with the use of brick and stone, with pilasters and elaborate windows incorporating cartouches and moulded stone swags. Each is further embellished by a shaped gable with a roundel window or similar decorative features. A slightly smaller example is the Straw House on Spicer Street, St Albans (Fig 76). This Italianate-style plait warehouse may be diminutive in scale when compared to Luton examples, but a considerable effort has been made to make the building visually impressive. Similarly, even the smaller warehouses in Luton demonstrate many of the designs favoured by their larger counterparts (Fig 77).

Figure 74 (above)
50 Guildford Street, Luton. The fronts of the buildings often form a stark contrast with the utilitarian sides or backs of the factories – money was only spent where it would be seen. In this case, the late 19th-century plait warehouse of Durler & Suter utilised red brick, terracotta and stone dressings to create a highly decorated façade in a hybrid Queen Anne Revival style characterised by the use of a shaped gable flanked by volutes, containing a terracotta roundel with prominent stone voussoirs, with moulded terracotta swags and tympana above many of the windows.
[DP141938]

Figure 75 (left)
Henry Durler & Son's hat factory and warehouse at 40 Guildford Street, Luton. Built in 1905 using a cast-iron frame it was designed with a number of neo-Jacobean elements including the obelisks either side of the gable, but also Queen Anne Revival touches such as the swags above the attic window. It is especially notable for its two-storey showroom front, a giant arcade serving to distinguish the showroom and offices from the functional factory element on the floors above.
[DP146078]

Figure 76 (above left)
The Straw House, Spicer Street, St Albans. Although smaller in scale than many of the central Luton hat factories and warehouses, this Italianate plait warehouse nonetheless demonstrates many of the same features in terms of plan, design and decoration – including a raised ground-floor showroom with basement below.
[DP153589]

Figure 77 (above right)
A pair of small millinery warehouses at 10–12 Wellington Street, Luton. Although small, these buildings display considerable attention to detail and investment in the construction materials, again with Queen Anne Revival touches such as the swags and the shaped aprons beneath the attic windows.
[DP154595]

The onset of the First World War saw the export market greatly reduced and engineering works supplying the war effort drew skilled staff and raw materials away from the trade. Nonetheless, the hatting industry did survive, adapting to meet the needs of a changing world. The result was progressively more rationalised building designs, with a focus on efficiency and best use of space. The new factories increasingly amalgamated the previously largely separate activities of making, trimming and finishing in one place, and thus what has been called the 'millinery trade' commenced.

To accommodate the changing requirements of the industry longer properties emerged which had a central core of offices, stairway, lift and often a lightwell, to the front and rear of which large open rooms, uninterrupted by even a central column, were used for production (Fig 78). This differed from earlier designs by turning the rooms on their axes – many of the earlier

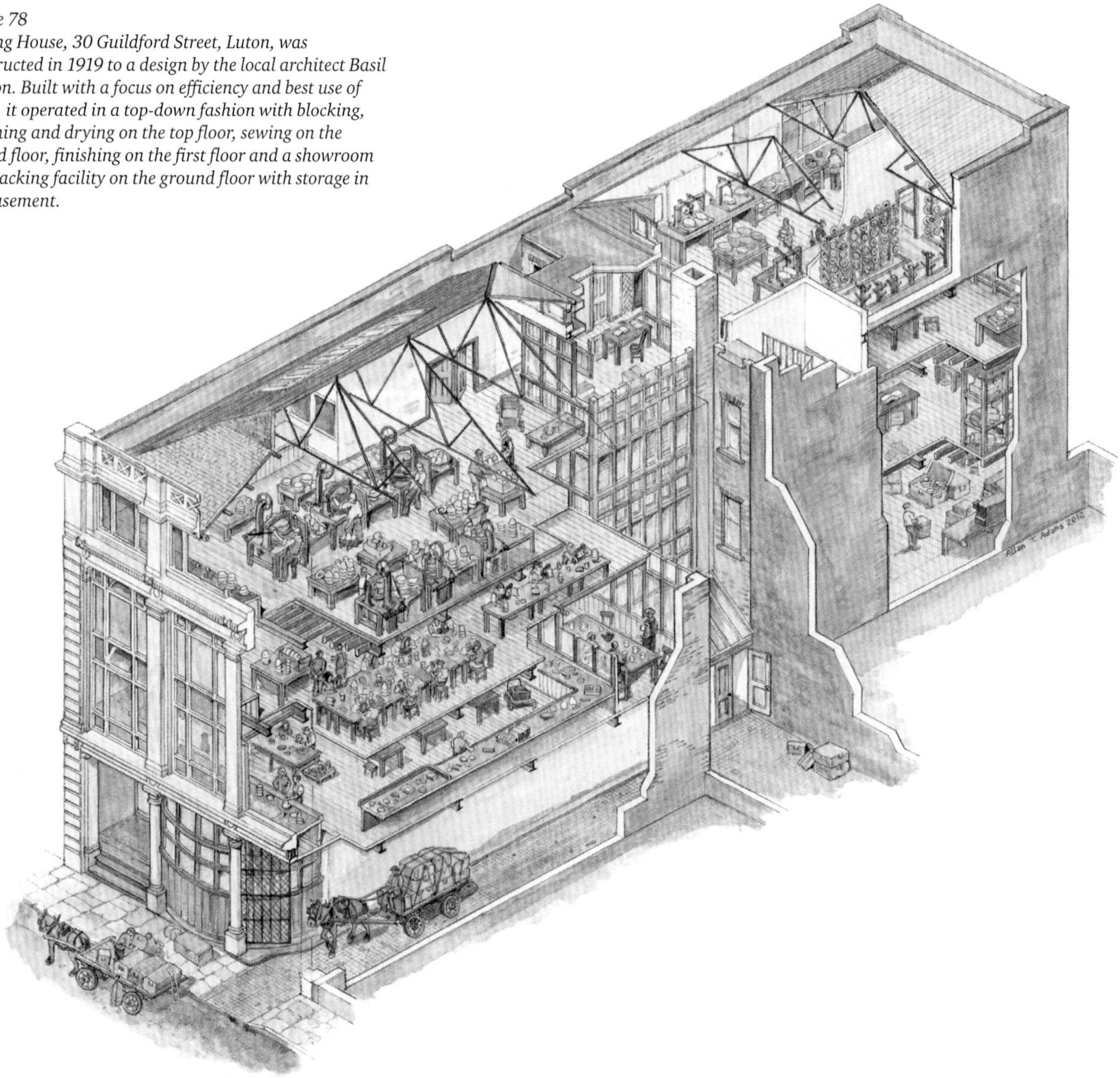

Figure 78
Stirling House, 30 Guildford Street, Luton, was constructed in 1919 to a design by the local architect Basil Deacon. Built with a focus on efficiency and best use of space, it operated in a top-down fashion with blocking, stiffening and drying on the top floor, sewing on the second floor, finishing on the first floor and a showroom and packing facility on the ground floor with storage in the basement.

Figure 79
Linda Kilpatrick – Linda worked as a sewer in Luton in the 1960s, a time when the industry continued to employ a substantial number of people. This photograph of her at a wedding was taken during the time she worked at J Collett's factory in Guildford Street.
[Courtesy of Linda Kilpatrick]

premises also had two rooms on the ground floor, but flanking the main entrance with a stairway to the extreme left or right. The new layout allowed for better circulation between rooms and floors, with the added benefit of relocating the dirtier processes to the rear of the building and well away from any visitors. It also enabled greater rationalisation in manufacture, the large factories operating in a top-down fashion, with each floor specialising in one particular aspect of the industry. The way in which these buildings operated is perhaps best explained through the memories of Linda Kilpatrick (née Greenwood) (Figs 79 and 80):

> In June 1962 I finished school at the age of 15 and applied for a job at J Collett's on Guildford Street. The hat factory was arranged over four floors and production began on the third floor which was set up for blocking and cutting. The men who worked up there were constantly surrounded by hot steam and the smell of wet woollen felt – the steam blocking was restricted to the top floor as it minimised the mess caused by the steam to the walls and ceiling. After blocking any excess felt was cut away from around the brim and the men were always surrounded by mounds of woollen scraps.
>
> The second floor was the sewing machining floor and there were always carts full of hats waiting in line to be delivered to each machine section – there were several sections on the machine floor, each undertaking a specific task under the supervision of a foreman or woman. Paper tickets hung off the sides of the carts with specific orders and instructions that we had to follow. In summer I worked in the 'box' machine section, where a line of boxy sewing machines were bolted to long industrial tables. A wooden block in the shape of a crown and brim sat at my left side and I would curve the straw into a neat circle and then begin chain stitching while working the straw into the shape of the block. When the crown looked close to the size of the block I removed it from the machine to check my sizing. Once I knew it was right, I placed it back on the machine until the brim looked complete and then tried it on the block again.
>
> A quick last go on the machine curved the edge of the brim and I would add the hat to the stack of finished hats beside me. When my orders

7
5
LUTON

Figure 80 (opposite)
The sewing machine floor of J Collett's – this photograph was taken at the time when Linda was working in the factory but she is not pictured.
[Luton Culture/The Luton News]

were complete I restacked them into another cart. The hats would then be taken down to the first floor which was set up for trimming and packing. Tables sat in rows with girls and ladies sitting all around, trimming hats by hand. Trimming was also outsourced to homeworkers who would come in several times a week to collect or drop off their orders. Once finished and inspected, the hats would be packed in tissue paper ready for shipping.

The ground floor housed the showroom and offices. Buyers made frequent trips to the showroom to see the latest collections and the director, Mr Sanders, would often take them on a tour of the factory.

When designing the factories which emerged following the First World War, architects eschewed the elaborate Queen Anne Revival and neo-Jacobean styles in favour of neo-Classical and neo-Georgian styles, which were now more fashionable. Stirling House, 30 Guildford Street, Luton (Fig 81), erected in 1919 with concrete render on a rigidly geometric façade, is a fine example of neo-Classical commercial design. It bears a strong similarity to a pair of 'daylight' hat factories built for F E Shoosmith & Son Ltd at 57–61 Guildford Street, Luton (Fig 82), where, unusually for a neo-Classical design of

Figure 81 (right)
The boxed showroom window, neo-Classical inspired white render, droplets, Doric columns, paterae and rusticated pilasters of Stirling House all serve to distinguish it from other hat factories and warehouses in Luton town centre.
[DP146068]

Figure 82 (far right)
The former F E Shoosmith & Son Ltd factory at 57–61 Guildford Street, Luton, has strong similarities to Stirling House. Built in the 1930s it has a concrete frame and is finished in a pared down neo-Classical style with some Art Deco details. Although the architect is unknown both buildings were commissioned by the builder W G Dunham who had close links with Basil Deacon, so it seems likely that it is his design.
[DP157638]

Figure 83
The former Vyse, Sons and Co Ltd factory on Bute Street, Luton, is unusual in having neo-Georgian inspired sash windows set within an otherwise industrial 'daylight' factory of c *1930. Such buildings normally have large, metal-framed windows to maximise the amount of natural light.*
[DP141920]

the 1920s, the ground floor is dominated by bow windows glazed in the moderne style.

The four-storey Vyse factory built at 47–53 Bute Street, Luton (Fig 83), in the early 1930s adopted a neo-Georgian idiom which is somewhat at odds with the industrial form of the building. The windows, instead of being metal-framed, are small-paned wooden sashes, separated by horizontal metal panels masking the floor levels and displaying, in the narrow central bay, the letter 'V'.

A few smaller-scale factories were built along the same lines, such as 22a–b Guildford Street (Fig 84) which is a noteworthy building in its own right – marked by its symmetrical plan form and geometrical street front elevation. This two-and-a-half-storey plait warehouse was built in the neo-Georgian style of the early 1930s.

No new hat factories were built in the Luton area following the Second World War and very few substantial alterations were made to the existing structures. The steady decline of the industry had begun and companies were, on the whole, beginning to contract rather than expand or invest in new premises. Accordingly, most of the buildings relating to the hat industry were built in a short period of 50 years, between *c* 1880 and 1930, when the industry was at its peak.

Figure 84
22a–b Guildford Street, Luton, an unusual pair of neo-Georgian plait warehouses of the early 1930s.
[DP146064]

London and its connections with the Luton hat industry

The hat trade in Luton has strong links to London, both geographically and economically. Vyse, one of the first large firms to establish a factory in Luton, was based in London and many other companies with warehouses or stores in London similarly chose to base their factories in Luton and St Albans where space, supply of materials and expertise were all plentiful.

However, a number of hat factories did exist in London itself and an area known as 'Hatters' Paradise', home to a concentration of fur-felt factories, was to be found on the South Bank, between Blackfriars Road and Tower Bridge Road in a narrow band close to the Thames. To the north, a second area between London Wall and Cheapside hosted the offices and warehouses of a number of businesses with properties not only in London, but also Luton and St Albans. Unfortunately this area was very heavily bombed during the

Figure 85
The Mad Hatter Hotel on Stamford Street, London. Formerly part of the Tress & Co hat factory, this Italianate style building is the last remnant of a once vast site. [DP157575]

Second World War and has subsequently been extensively redeveloped, so little evidence remains.

Perhaps the most easily identified remnant of the London industry is The Mad Hatter Hotel (Fig 85) on Stamford Street, just off Blackfriars Road, formerly the office and showroom block of Tress & Co hat manufacturers. By 1914 the company also had a factory in Luton at the Albion Works on Albion Road – now the home of Walter Wright Ltd. The block is the surviving remnant of a once vast factory site which extended to the rear. Constructed in *c* 1875, the Italianate design and rusticated ground floor are reminiscent of many Luton warehouses of the same period.

The former hat factories on Dufferin Street are more utilitarian (Fig 86).

Figure 86
Warehouses on Dufferin Street, Islington, London. These reasonably plain buildings were used for the production and storage of hats which were then sold on through the more lavishly designed and decorated showrooms and retailers in central London.
[DP151009]

These rather plain buildings, which were surrounded by straw- and sewing-machine warehouses as well as box- and packing-case manufacturers, worked on the same basic principles and layouts as Luton examples, but appear to have played less of a public-facing role. They produced or stored hats which were then sold through more lavishly designed and decorated central showrooms and stores so it was not considered necessary to invest a large amount of money in their ornamentation.

A marked feature of the London industry was that many manufacturers sold their hats directly to the public through their own shops and a number of these have survived in the commercial heart of London. Erected in 1887–8, 105–9 Oxford Street was the factory and shop of Henry Heath Ltd (Fig 87). This fine building has a highly decorated façade and, although the frieze depicting the processes of hat making is sadly obscured by the current shopfront, the true nature of the building is hinted at by the use of stone beavers as finials on the gables – a reference to fur-felt production. The rear of the building, fronting Hollen Street, is unmistakably designed as a factory building – and has the words 'Hat Factory. Henry Heath. Oxford Street' in stone relief bands across the façade (Fig 88). The overall emphasis of the building, with its elaborate façade along Oxford Street, is very much on retail, yet the factory aspect, although clearly industrial in aesthetic, is still designed to impress.

Not far away, at 16–18 Ramillies Street, is an early 20th-century hat factory designed by the architect E K Purchase. This building is similar to the early 20th-century hat factories seen in Luton – with a raised ground-floor showroom over a basement, and space for manufacturing processes above lit by large, cast-iron framed windows. By 1921 it was home to Edward C Churchill Ltd, a ladies' hat manufacturer, and later to the Glenster Hat Company.

Figure 87
Henry Heath's hat factory at 105–9 Oxford Street, London. This lavishly designed building of 1887–8 has a public-facing showroom on Oxford Street, the frieze depicting the process of hat making now obscured by later shopfronts. The only visible connection with the hat trade is the use of stone beavers as finials on the gables – a reference to the fur-felt trade.
[BL12678]

Figure 88
Accessed from Hollen Street, the rear of Henry Heath's hat factory could easily be mistaken as being an entirely separate building – the difference in style, materials and scale is striking.
[DP151004]

STRATHMORE
HOTEL
NO PARKING
IN FRONT OF GATES
24 HOUR ACCESS
REQUIRED

6

Conservation and the management of change

As this book has demonstrated, the hat industry has left behind a rich and varied inventory of buildings. Although the highest density of these buildings may be found in Luton itself, it is clear that the industry played a significant role in shaping the appearance of towns and villages for miles around. Remarkably, given the extent to which the industry has declined, a number of firms continue to use their historic premises, employing traditional techniques, skills and machinery. It is testament to the flexible designs of these buildings that they remain fit for purpose 100 years or more after first opening.

The domestic nature of much of the early industry, in buildings frequently subject to change and demolition, means this legacy is necessarily patchy and the picture today is incomplete. But, notwithstanding the loss of many of the domestic buildings, the industrial phases of the latter half of the 19th and early decades of the 20th centuries are well represented. We know that many buildings of considerable historic and architectural interest have been lost, but the surviving buildings give us a clear understanding of an industry which thrived in the years between 1880 and 1930.

The fragmented nature of the early hat industry in Luton and the surrounding area often resulted in buildings that were quite small in scale, integrated into the urban grain of the communities in which they were built and with limited architectural pretensions. The modest nature of some of these buildings is an inherent and significant part of their character, though it has, perhaps, caused them to be overlooked and undervalued in the past. Towards the end of the 19th century, however, both the scale of the premises and their architectural ambitions increased – resulting in a collection of buildings that has significant presence in the streetscape (Fig 89). These later properties are often considerable in size, designed to make best use of the available space and providing employment for as many as 400 employees on site, with hundreds more homeworkers associated with any one firm.

The unassuming scale of the early buildings, coupled with the frame construction employed in the later, larger buildings (Fig 90), means that most buildings of the hat industry are readily adaptable for other uses, both commercial and residential in nature. However, the contraction of local industry and the recent economic climate has resulted in a number of these buildings languishing empty or underused and at risk of further decline (Fig 91).

47 Guildford Street, built in the 1840s, is believed to be the earliest surviving hat factory in Luton and is Grade II listed. It is under threat from proposals for the redevelopment of Luton town centre – some of which would seek to demolish it.

Figure 89
Factories and warehouses constructed towards the end of the 19th and into the 20th century tend to be elaborate in design and make a significant contribution to the character of the area, such as the former Austin & Co factory at 37–39 Guildford Street, Luton, of c *1914 which was built in a bold Edwardian baroque style.*
[DP146095]

Figure 90
Detail of cast-iron frame, Plaiters' Lea, Luton.
[David Grech]

Figure 91
The former Barford & Sons' hat factory at 7 King Street, Luton, suffered a fire in July 2007 which destroyed the roof and the upper floor, causing smoke and heat damage to the rest of the building. It has been left to decay with no attempt to repair or restore the building.
[DP154593]

Whilst the reduced pressure for redevelopment in recent years has provided a breathing space in which we have been able to research and evaluate the importance of this built heritage, it is expected that development pressures within the region will increase over time and the future of these buildings must be addressed.

In March 2012 the Government issued its new National Planning Policy Framework (NPPF) which brought together all the previous, disparate guidance issued to help inform the planning process. While one of the main aims behind the introduction of the NPPF was to promote sustainable development, it also includes a number of policies specific to the historic environment that look at the role historic buildings can assume in place shaping, and reinforcing local character and identity.

At a local level in Luton the significance of the hat industry's legacy has been acknowledged through the designation of Plaiters' Lea as a conservation area. Strangely, the High Town Conservation Area excludes most of the buildings of the hat industry in that area. Elsewhere, such as at Dunstable, although buildings of the hat industry again lie within a conservation area, their role is largely underplayed. A review of the boundaries of these conservation areas would identify additional hat industry buildings nearby that might be brought within their protection, and the north side of the western part of Guildford Street at Luton's Plaiters' Lea is one such example; a similar review should also be undertaken for the High Town and Rothesay Conservation Areas in Luton.

Some buildings, but only a minority, have additional protection afforded by inclusion on the national heritage list for England, and it is hoped that the improved understanding of the hat industry and its buildings will, over time, result in more buildings being added to the list. Furthermore, English Heritage has recently published guidance for local authorities on preparing local lists of buildings of architectural and historic interest within their area, and many of the other surviving buildings from the hat industry might benefit from inclusion on a local list.

The careful application of the policies within the NPPF and Local Plans will enable the surviving buildings of the hat industry to be retained for appropriate new uses, while at the same time ensuring their inherent character is respected and their original role can continue to be discerned and understood. This will require a sympathetic approach to the process of adaptation, ensuring that original windows and doors are maintained (or reinstated where lost) along with the finer grain of detail recorded in distinctive plaques, datestones and lettering. Original external walling and roofing should also be preserved along with traditional cast-iron rainwater goods, chimney stacks and the like. Where extensions are necessary to support a new use they should be proportionate to the original building and appropriately sited so as not to dominate it.

Managing change to the buildings of the hat industry and encouraging sympathetic redevelopment presents challenges. Cases in point include Paul Walser's former hat factory on the corner of Midland Road and Dudley Street in High Town, Luton (Fig 92), dating from the interwar period and now converted to offices. It lies outside the boundaries of the nearby High Town Conservation Area and the conversion included the provision of three additional floors set back behind the original parapet. While the provision of a single additional storey would not have adversely impacted on the character of the building, the three additional floors are out of proportion with the original four-storey building and have resulted in an unsatisfactory visual imbalance. In addition, while the replacement windows make a token reference to the original metal casements, they again result in an erosion of the character and appearance of the original building.

By contrast, the recently restored and converted factory at 35 John Street (Fig 93) in the Plaiters' Lea Conservation Area is much more successful in respecting the character and appearance of the original building that dates from the same interwar period.

Conservation of the buildings of the hat industry is not just about the survival of individual buildings. Their collective value is an important component of their conservation and, therefore, when major proposals for

Figure 92
Paul Walser's former hat factory on the corner of Midland Road and Dudley Street in High Town, Luton, has suffered from unsympathetic additions which are out of proportion with the original building.
[DP154618]

Figure 93
An example of sympathetic alterations to a hat factory at 35 John Street, Luton.
[DP141942]

urban regeneration are being considered it is essential that an early and proper consideration of this value informs any master-planning process. In the past wholesale demolition of blocks of buildings has been permitted, particularly within the Plaiters' Lea Conservation Area (Fig 94) and, while the individual buildings removed may have been considered to be of lesser architectural interest and in a poor state of repair, the continued erosion of these hat industry structures is not just a matter of regret; it represents the depletion of a finite resource that cannot be replaced. In conservation areas there is a presumption in favour of the retention of buildings that make a positive contribution to the character and appearance of the area. Furthermore, the NPPF includes specific guidance to local planning authorities to ignore deliberate neglect or damage to heritage assets when making decisions

Figure 94
While removal of inappropriate post-war buildings may provide the opportunity for replacement buildings of better quality, cleared sites can equally result in blight that, in turn, may remove the incentive to maintain vulnerable buildings that positively contribute to conservation areas.
[David Grech]

concerning their future. It is important that this presumption in favour of retention, and the guidance on deliberate neglect, is properly understood and used when assessing future proposals for demolition. Where buildings have already been lost, consideration should be given to reinstating the historic grain and urban form as part of any redevelopment proposals. It is hoped that any future schemes, including the planned 'facelift' of Luton's Bute Street area by the Town Team in conjunction with local businesses and the University of Bedfordshire, will be undertaken with due consideration of the impact that any work will have on the significance and setting of the buildings, and with a view to enhancing their heritage values wherever possible. In these ways the built history of the hat industry will survive for the benefit of future generations.

Notes

1 Hansard HC Deb, 15 July 1999, vol 335, columns 682–90.

2 House of Commons Parliamentary Papers. 'Brought by message from the Lords, 9th March 1818. Report of the Lords committees on the poor laws: dated 10 July 1817. Ordered, by the House of Commons, to be Printed, 1 June 1818.'

3 House of Commons Parliamentary Papers. 'Children's Employment Commission (1862). Second report of the commissioners. With appendix. Presented to both Houses of Parliament by Command of Her Majesty. London, HMSO, 1864.

4 House of Commons Parliamentary Papers. 'Schools Inquiry Commission. Vol. XII. South Midland division. Special reports of assistant commissioners, and digests of information received. Presented to both Houses of Parliament by Command of Her Majesty. London, HMSO, 1868.'

5 Bunker, 1999, 33.

6 Bigmore, 1979, 220.

7 Austin, 1871, 18.

8 Dony, 1942, 111.

9 House of Commons Parliamentary Papers. 'Children's Employment Commission. Second report of the commissioners. Trades and manufactures. Presented to both Houses of Parliament by Command of Her Majesty. London, HMSO, 1843.'

10 *The Times*, 12 March 1930, 11, column A.

11 Smith, 1972, 60.

References and further reading

Austin, T G 1871 *The Straw Plaiting and Straw Hat and Bonnet Trade with a Digest of the Recent Census for the Luton District*. Luton: Patrick O'Doherty

Bevan, D 1992 'Buildings of the Luton hatting industry in Luton and four other centres'. Unpublished Architectural Association Building Conservation Course Thesis

Bigmore, P 1979 *The Making of The English Landscape: The Bedfordshire and Huntingdonshire Landscape*. London: Hodder & Stoughton

Bunker, S 1999 *Strawopolis: Luton transformed 1840–1876. Bedfordshire Historical Record Society* **78**. Bedford: Bedfordshire Historical Record Society

Bunyan, J 2003 *The Pilgrim's Progress*. Oxford: Oxford University Press (first published 1678)

Curran, J, 2003 *Straw Hats and Bonnets*. Dunstable and District Local History Society, Old Trades of Dunstable **5**. Dunstable: The Book Castle

Dony, J G 1942 *A History of the Straw Hat Industry*. Luton: Gibbs, Bamforth & Co

Dony, J G 1946 'The hat industry'. *Studies in Industrial Organization* **3**, Silverman, H A (ed), 155–98

Dyer, J and Dony, J G 1975 *The Story of Luton*, 3 edn. Luton: White Crescent Press

Freeman, C 1964 *Luton and the Hat Industry*, rev edn. Luton: The Corporation of Luton Museum and Art Gallery

Goodman, F 1898 'How the railways deal with special classes of traffic – Luton straw hats'. *The Railway Magazine* **3**, 451–67

Goose, N 2006 'How saucy did it make the poor? The straw plait and hat trades, illegitimate fertility and the family in nineteenth-century Hertfordshire'. *History* **91**, 530–56

Horn, P 1974 'Child workers in the pillow lace and straw plait trades in Victorian Buckinghamshire and Bedfordshire'. *The Historical Journal* **17**, 779–96

Pevsner, N 1968 *Bedfordshire, Huntingdon and Peterborough* (Pevsner Architectural Guides: Buildings of England). Harmondsworth: Penguin Books Ltd

Smith, T P 1972 'House-types connected with the Luton hat industry: A preliminary survey'. *Industrial Archaeology* **9**, 58–64

Online

Carmichael, K, McOmish, D and Grech, D 2011 *Plaiters' Lea Conservation Area, Luton*. English Heritage Research Department Report Series, no 69-2011. PDF available at http://research.english-heritage.org.uk/report/?15021

Graham, K 2010 *The Barford Brothers' Dye and Bleach Works*. English Heritage Research Department Report Series, no 83-2010. PDF available at http://research.english-heritage.org.uk/report/?14934

The Bedfordshire and Luton Extensive Urban Survey, 2005. Available at http://archaeologydataservice.ac.uk/archives/view/bedsluton_eus_2006/

The National Planning Policy Framework, Dept of Communities and Local Government, 2012. Available at https://www.gov.uk/government/publications/national-planning-policy-framework--2

Other titles in the Informed Conservation series

Alston Moor: Buildings in a North Pennines landscape
Lucy Jessop and Matthew Whitfield, with Andrew Davison, 2013
ISBN 9781848021174

Ancoats: Cradle of industrialisation
Michael E Rose with Keith Falconer and Julian Holder, 2011
ISBN 9781848020276

Behind the Veneer: The South Shoreditch furniture trade and its buildings
Joanna Smith and Ray Rogers, 2006
ISBN 9781873592960

Berwick-upon-Tweed: Three places, two nations, one town
Adam Menuge with Catherine Dewar, 2009
ISBN 9781848020290

The Birmingham Jewellery Quarter: An introduction and guide
John Cattell and Bob Hawkins, 2000
ISBN 9781850747772

Bridport and West Bay: The buildings of the flax and hemp industry
Mike Williams, 2006
ISBN 9781873592861

Building a Better Society: Liverpool's historic institutional buildings
Colum Giles, 2008
ISBN 9781873592908

Built on Commerce: Liverpool's central business district
Joseph Sharples and John Stonard, 2008
ISBN 9781905624348

Built to Last? The buildings of the Northamptonshire boot and shoe industry
Kathryn A Morrison with Ann Bond, 2004
ISBN 9781873592793

Defending Scilly
Mark Bowden and Allan Brodie, 2011
ISBN 9781848020436

England's Schools: History, architecture and adaptation
Elain Harwood, 2010
ISBN 9781848020313

English Garden Cities: An introduction
Mervyn Miller, 2010
ISBN 9781848020511

Gateshead: Architecture in a changing English urban landscape
Simon Taylor and David Lovie, 2004
ISBN 9781873592762

Manchester's Northern Quarter
Simon Taylor and Julian Holder, 2008
ISBN 9781873592847

Manchester: The warehouse legacy – An introduction and guide
Simon Taylor, Malcolm Cooper and P S Barnwell, 2002
ISBN 9781873592670

Manningham: Character and diversity in a Bradford suburb
Simon Taylor and Kathryn Gibson, 2010
ISBN 9781848020306

Margate's Seaside Heritage
Nigel Barker, Allan Brodie, Nick Dermott, Lucy Jessop and Gary Winter, 2007
ISBN 9781905624669

Newcastle's Grainger Town: An urban renaissance
Fiona Cullen and David Lovie, 2003
ISBN 9781873592779

'One Great Workshop': The buildings of the Sheffield metal trades
Nicola Wray, Bob Hawkins and Colum Giles, 2001
ISBN 9781873592663

Ordinary Landscapes, Special Places: Anfield, Breckfield and the growth of Liverpool's suburbs
Adam Menuge, 2008
ISBN 9781873592892

Places of Health and Amusement: Liverpool's historic parks and gardens
Katy Layton-Jones and Robert Lee, 2008
ISBN 9781873592915

Plymouth: Vision of a modern city
Jeremy Gould, 2010
ISBN 9781848020504

Religion and Place in Leeds
John Minnis with Trevor Mitchell, 2007
ISBN 9781905624485

Stourport-on-Severn: Pioneer town of the canal age
Colum Giles, Keith Falconer, Barry Jones and Michael Taylor, 2007
ISBN 9781905624362

Weymouth's Seaside Heritage
Allan Brodie, Colin Ellis, David Stuart and Gary Winter, 2008
ISBN 9781848020085

Further information on titles in the Informed Conservation series can be found on our website www. english-heritage.org.uk.
To order through EH Sales
Tel: 01235 465577
Fax: 01235 465556
Email: direct.order@marston.co.uk

Current

1 Marie-Louise Millinery, 110 Clarendon Road – milliner

2 K R Snoxell & Sons Ltd, 24–26 Clarendon Road – hat manufacturer

3 Olney Headwear Ltd, 106 Old Bedford Road – hat manufacturer

4 Ken Peirson & Son Ltd, 86 Old Bedford Road – hat manufacturer

5 W Fischer & Sons (Luton) Ltd (built as the stables for the Barford Brothers' dye works), 4a William Street – trimmings and accessories

6 Barford Brothers Ltd, 111 North Street – dye works, (*see* Fig 71)

7 Randall Ribbons, part of Ken Peirson & Son Ltd, 12 Frederick Street – trimmings and accessories

8 Boon & Lane Ltd, 7–11 Taylor Street – block makers

9 Walter Wright Ltd , 29 Albion Road – hat manufacturer, (*see* Fig 62)

Former

10 69 Havelock Road, (*see* Fig 45)

11 Marida Ltd, 1 Dudley Street

12 Paul Walser Ltd (aka Reslaw), corner of Midland Road and Dudley Street, (*see* Fig 92)

13 Formerly Durler & Suter, 50 Guildford Street, (*see* Fig 74)

14 F E Shoosmith & Son Ltd, 57–61 Guildford Street, (*see* Fig 82)

15 Henry Durler & Sons, 40 Guildford Street, (*see* Fig 75)

16 'The Hat Factory', formerly J & K Connor Ltd, Bute Street, (*see* Fig 63 and front cover)

17 Walter Gurney & Son Ltd, 64 Bute Street, (*see* Fig 73)

18 47 Guildford Street, (*see* Fig 55)

19 Stirling House, 30 Guildford Street, (*see* Figs 78 and 81)

20 Austin & Co, 37–39 Guildford Street, (*see* Fig 89)

21 22a–b, Guildford Street, (*see* Fig 84)

22 Former stable, to the rear of 43 Guildford Street (*see* Fig 54)

23 Vyse, Sons and Co Ltd, 47–53 Bute Street, (*see* Fig 83)

24 16 John Street, (*see* Fig 65)

25 35 John Street, (*see* Fig 93)

26 10–12 Wellington Street, (*see* Fig 77)

27 25 Wellington Street, formerly part of J J Webdale & Sons, (*see* Fig 61)

28 Barford & Sons, 7 King Street, (*see* Fig 91)

29 2 George Street West, (*see* Fig 60)

30 Stevens & Gee Ltd, 30 King Street

31 A Healey, 71 Buxton Road, (*see* Fig 41)

32 Stygall & Grundy, 73 Buxton Road, (*see* Fig 41)

33 84 Princess Street, (*see* Fig 44)

34 81 Dumfries Street, (*see* Fig 43)

This map shows only a selection of those buildings with a documented connection to the hat industry. It is not intended to show the industry as it was at any one date, and not all of the buildings would have been in active use at any given time.

Back cover
A lady models a novelty hat featuring a horse race. Although clearly not designed for the mass-market, pieces such as this were a way for hat makers to demonstrate their skills and creativity.
[Luton Culture/The Luton News]